PELICAN BOOKS

THE COMPREHENSIVE SCHOOL

Robin Pedley attended a village school in Swaledale, Yorks., until, at fourteen, he was appointed a pupil teacher at a starting salary of £5 p.a. He went to Richmond Grammar School to prepare for training college entrance, but instead won scholarships to Durham University. There he gained prizes in archaeology and modern history, a research fellowship and a Ph.D. He has played soccer in the Northern League and cricket in the Yorkshire Council, and has taught in schools, training colleges, and universities.

Since 1949 Professor Pedley has written, lectured, and broadcast extensively, both in England and abroad, on his proposals for abolishing the 11+ examination and substituting a comprehensive, two-tier organization of secondary schools – a plan whose main thesis has been adopted by a large number of local education authorities. His book *Comprehensive Education: A New Approach* (1956) attracted widespread notice; it was quoted freely in the House of Commons debates, and led to a conference between the author and the Minister of Education on Professor Pedley's proposals.

Professor Pedley has studied and lectured on education in various parts of the world, notably Canada, Israel and Japan. He is a member of the Secretary of State's Consultative committee on Research into Comprehensive Education.

D1412809

ROBIN PEDLEY

The Comprehensive School

SECOND EDITION

PENGUIN BOOKS

Penguin Books Ltd, Harmondsworth, Middlesex, England
Penguin Books Inc., 7110 Ambassador Road, Baltimore, Maryland 21207, U.S.A.
Penguin Books Australia Ltd, Ringwood, Victoria, Australia

—

First published 1963
Reprinted with minor revisions 1964
Reprinted (with revisions) 1966, 1967
Revised edition 1969
Reprinted 1970, 1972

—

—

Made and printed in Great Britain
by C. Nicholls & Company Ltd
Set in Linotype Pilgrim

Contents

Author's Note

MY subject is the comprehensive school in England, Wales and the Isle of Man. A study of schools of similar type in other parts of the world would fill many volumes, and I have therefore looked elsewhere only for occasional illustration and comparison.

In the six years which have elapsed since this book was first published great changes have taken place. The Government has adopted the comprehensive principle for its schools (though not, as yet, for further and higher education) and as a result the State school system is being transformed. To take account of these momentous developments the book has now been extensively revised and largely rewritten. Its philosophy, however, remains unchanged.

1969

Acknowledgements

I AM indebted to the many head teachers and the officers of local education authorities and the Department of Education and Science who in countless ways have helped my study of secondary education over the years. Generous invitations from several Canadian School Boards and Universities, from the Israeli Ministry of Education and Culture, from the Ministries of Education and Universities of Thailand and Japan, and from the British Council, made possible my study at first hand of schools and teacher training in those countries. I have greatly benefited, too, from the frequent exchange of critical ideas with parents, teachers, lay members of education committees, university scholars, and others – especially those whose views have differed from mine.

I wish to record my gratitude to my father and mother, whose sacrifices made my own education possible; to my sister and brothers for their invaluable support, criticism and advice over the years; to my wife for her interest and unfailing encouragement; and to my children whose experience, first in an unstreamed primary school in Leicestershire and then in a comprehensive secondary school in Dorset, has been a daily reminder of what this book is really all about.

1. 'A New Society'?

'IN spite of the virtual abolition of poverty, in spite of the rise there has been in the rewards of labour, in spite of the fact that ... the great bulk of the nation now regards itself as middle-class, Britain is still a jealous and divided nation.'[1]

England in the 1960s was an aristocratic society, not a democratic one. That is the main fact to be realized if its system of education is to be fully understood. As we enter the 1970s great changes are afoot but in important ways the balance of social forces remains conservative.

At one time it was assumed that quality went with noble birth. Then wealth replaced birth as the *sine qua non*. Both criteria live on in English society today, but ability is rapidly replacing them as the key to a position of power. Because the term 'aristocracy' has become entangled in people's minds with the idea of an unjustly privileged class, the word 'meritocracy' has been coined to express more clearly the new system of government by the ablest people. One hundred years after the first great Elementary Education Act the Englishman still does not believe in equality. What he wants is equal opportunity to be unequal.

We have, then, a society made up of different classes. Because many top people still owe their eminence to birth and inherited wealth, now increasingly felt to be 'unfair', there is much pressure to reform the conditions of membership, making personal ability the measuring-rod, and to ease movement from one class to another. Such reforms will of course strengthen the class system. They are completely at variance with the quite different aim of a minority (though a growing minority) of idealists: to abolish the class system altogether.

1. *The Times*, leading article of 13 July 1961, 'A New Society'.

Education in England still mirrors the English social system. There are three main routes through early life, each with its social ranking order. Transfer from one route to another can occur in special cases, and the possibility of such transfer acts as a social safety valve; but a child launched on the second or third route must combine marked ability with good fortune, if he **is** not to follow that track to the end. For those interested in athletics these routes may be likened to the lanes in which the 400 metres is run, with one vital exception: there is no staggered start to ensure an equal chance for all competitors.

Route One, normally open to the children of parents who can afford to pay large fees, takes a boy from private kindergarten (perhaps four to eight) to preparatory school (eight to thirteen), 'public' or independent school (thirteen to eighteen), and, provided he has the modest ability required to matriculate, Oxford University or Cambridge University. Of all thirteen-year-olds in England and Wales, seven per cent are on the inside lane: five per cent in recognized independent schools, two per cent in direct-grant grammar schools.

Direct-grant schools are independent of local authorities, but receive a grant direct from the Department of Education and Science. In addition to fee-payers, they must take at least twenty-five per cent of their pupils from local primary schools; these pupils are selected on the results of the eleven-plus examination. There are only 178 direct-grant grammar schools in England and Wales.

The leading 'public' schools now set quite exacting entrance tests for nearly all their pupils – a further sign that ability is slowly coming to be the first requirement for membership of the top social group. Likewise, at Oxford and Cambridge, severe competition from brilliant grammar school pupils limits the number of places which may be quietly reserved for the ordinary scions of famous fathers.

Even so, longstanding personal contacts among particular colleges and 'public' and preparatory schools still ensure that the requirement of great academic ability, demanded of most applicants, may be remitted in favoured cases. The experience of Winston Churchill eighty years ago is not wholly out of date. This is his own account of an examination he sat for admission to a famous independent school:

I wrote my name at the top of the page. I put down the number of the question: '1': After much reflection I put a bracket round it thus: '(1)'. But thereafter I could not think of anything connected with it that was either relevant or true. Incidentally there arrived from nowhere in particular a blot and several smudges. I gazed for two whole hours at this sad spectacle: and then merciful ushers collected my piece of foolscap with all the others and carried it up to the Headmaster's table. It was from these slender indications of scholarship that Mr Welldon drew the conclusion that I was worthy to pass into Harrow.[1]

Route Two is much more conditioned by the new accent on ability, though not wholly so. In 1967 thirty-two per cent of each age group were in this middle lane – seventeen per cent in local grammar schools, two per cent in technical schools, and thirteen per cent in comprehensive schools.[2] It has normally taken a boy from the local primary school to the grammar school after passing the eleven-plus qualifying examination, and thence, after eventually gaining two or three advanced-level passes in the General Certificate of Education (GCE), to a provincial university. A brilliant minority force their way into Oxford or Cambridge. Others may go to a technical college or direct into commerce or industry. The successful local

1. *My Early Life* (Odhams Press, 1934).
2. Twenty-one per cent in comprehensive schools by 1968.

school boy's normal target, however, is coming to be a place at a provincial university; and as more of these places are provided, as industry requires more educated personnel, and as therefore more boys and girls stay at school until eighteen to prepare for full-time education, it will increasingly be so.

Route Three is mainly for those who fail to get into a grammar or comprehensive school at eleven: in 1967 fifty-eight per cent in 'secondary modern', other secondary and all-age schools, one per cent in other independent schools, and one per cent in special schools.[1] Most go to 'modern' schools and normally leave at fifteen or sixteen. In some of the 3,000 'modern' schools in England and Wales it is possible for the cleverer pupils to sit for GCE at ordinary level, and many more take examinations at a lower level. A minority go on to gain a technical college qualification by long and arduous part-time study. The vast majority, however, become the hewers of wood and drawers of water of our graded society. The Certificate of Secondary Education was introduced in 1965 for those pupils who were unable to take GCE. This new certificate has many excellent features, but it does refine the educational ranking order.

This, of course, is an over-simplified picture. Not all boys from independent schools go to Oxford or Cambridge, and far fewer girls; for women are only grudgingly accepted in those very conservative communities. An increasing number of very able grammar and comprehensive school pupils are entering Oxford and Cambridge. On the other hand, there is little chance to move from the middle to the inside lane at any earlier stage. At the other end of the scale it has been possible for a few 'modern' school children to

1. 7% (route 1) + 32% (route 2) + 60% (route 3) = 99%. Small fractions, omitted in calculating to the nearest whole number, account for the missing 1%.

secure transfer to the grammar school at thirteen or six-teen, and the odd one has even reached a provincial University.

Such exceptions blur the hard outlines of a three-class system of education. They are necessary to make such a system tolerable. They provide escape channels for the exceptionally able, but they do not seriously alter the main pattern; rather do they help to entrench it further. As the editor of *School and College* forthrightly stated: 'The whole issue is one of class ... for the English, more than others, believe in class and have taken the greatest pains to establish and protect it.'[1]

In his novel about the Civil Service in England, *Clerks in Lowly Orders*, Stuart Mitchel states Plato's ideas in modern terms. There are the men of gold, the administrative class who decide policy, drawn almost exclusively from the runners on the inside lane. There are the men of silver, the executive class, who interpret and implement that policy, drawn from those who have followed the less advantageous middle lane. And there are the men of brass, the clerical class who do the routine work, who have either lagged behind in the middle lane or hopelessly followed the out-side lane in the educational race. The Certificate of Secondary Education makes a last careful distinction between the men of brass and the men of dross: a timely incentive, this, to encourage the upward struggle among even the lowliest of us.

At present we are doing little to put an end to the advantages held by those who occupy the inside lane. The great argument in England, curiously enough, is almost entirely about ways and means of removing the line between the middle and the outside lanes which for most children is still drawn from the age of eleven onwards, and which has depended on the most celebrated, most unpopular, yet most

1. *School and College*, February 1962, p. 13.

potent feature of English education – the eleven-plus examination.

Selection at eleven[1]

The eleven-plus examination is a process of selection for places in grammar schools which may take anything from three months to three years to complete.[2] At its best it is perhaps the most thorough examination ever devised, and it is usually administered with meticulous fairness. It normally consists of four parts: (i) tests of intelligence; (ii) tests of attainment in English and Arithmetic; (iii) records of the child's work at primary school with teachers' recommendations; (iv) interviews, in borderline cases.

Intelligence tests produce a rating called the intelligence quotient, or I.Q. This is the child's mental age, as measured by the tests, expressed as a percentage of chronological age. Thus a child of ten whose mental age is twelve has an I.Q. of 120. A child of ten whose mental age is eight has an I.Q. of 80.

The proportion of children admitted to a grammar school varies according to the number of places available and the policy of the local education authority. It has been as low as ten per cent or as high as forty per cent of all the children for whom the local education authority is responsible. (Fee-payers at independent and direct-grant schools are excluded from these calculations.) The average for England and Wales has been twenty per cent. Children with I.Q.s of 120 and over usually qualify for places in grammar schools.

1. Cf. *Secondary School Selection*, ed. Vernon (Methuen, 1957), and *Procedures for the allocation of pupils in Secondary Education* (National Foundation for Educational Research, 1963).

2. I write in the present tense, because *Trends in Allocation Procedures* (N.F.E.R., 1969) shows that only 26 LEAs out of 163 had abandoned it by 1968, though 44 had dropped attainment tests.

Before 1955 or thereabouts, public confidence in the fairness and accuracy of the examination rested on the belief that intelligence tests could detect and measure inborn ability. In the middle fifties this belief was strongly challenged by such university teachers as Philip Vernon, Brian Simon, and John Daniels, who demonstrated conclusively that this was not so. None of the tests conceived and tried over the course of sixty years can satisfactorily distinguish natural talent from what has been learned. Heredity and environment are too closely entangled to be closely identified. This means that children from literate homes, with interested and helpful parents, have an enormous advantage over children from culturally poor homes where books are unknown and conversation is either limited or unprintable.

Children's attainment in English and mathematics is also greatly affected by such factors. Some parents spend hours helping their children to read. At the other extreme, there are parents who violently prevent their children from reading; in such homes books are hated or despised. Many parents are indifferent. Further, progress is much affected by health, attendance at school, and the luck of having a good or a bad class teacher there.

Surveys indicate that teachers' reports, taken as a whole, are just as valid as intelligence tests. But here too much depends on the judgement of individuals; one teacher's may be very good, another's poor. The intelligence test is more uniform and stable. Moreover the responsibility of deciding whether a child goes to the grammar school or not is one which few teachers relish. They know how fallible the available evidence must often be, how unpredictable the response of children to future stimuli.

Teachers' judgements may seem to be better than they really are, because grouping in the junior school itself helps to decide a child's success or failure at eleven-plus.

'Give a dog a bad name' is all too pertinent here. A child put in the 'A' or top stream at the age of seven finds himself in a stimulating environment. He is often also given one of the better teachers. Such a child may reasonably be expected to go on doing well and be selected for a grammar school. Conversely the child labelled 'C' at seven, in a much less stimulating environment, feeling inferior, and not infrequently put in the care of a poorer teacher, has little chance of success in the eleven-plus examination. So he goes, conscious of his failure, to a school commonly regarded as a school for failures, a school which often has both larger classes and a more limited range of courses than the grammar school. It takes an unusually gifted and/ or determined child to refuse to accept these handicaps, to fight and overcome them. How many accept with resignation the mark others have put on them, after only six years' schooling, cannot be fully known.

Finally, the interview, as an instrument of fine objective judgement among candidates already ranked close together, is fantastically unsound. No survey rates its validity high. Personal impressions in a short interview are much too haphazard, too liable to be influenced by chance remarks or by the child's speech, dress, and manners. This is undoubtedly the weakest part of the eleven-plus procedure. It does nothing to refine selection at the point where accuracy and refinement are most needed; and while superficially it may give an air of extra care to the business, in fact it lowers it from the plane of detached objective assessment to that of inexpert rough justice.

Disturbed by these failings, yet unwilling or feeling temporarily unable to abandon selection at eleven, some local authorities have modified the procedure in one way or another. Some have dropped intelligence tests, partly because the idea that they could distinguish inborn ability has been exploded, and partly because coaching in similar tests – much practised in some schools, not at all in others – can give the coached child an unfair advantage. Moreover, it is undesirable that these tests should figure as a regular time-consuming part of junior-school work, as has sometimes happened. On the other hand, despite their deficiencies, intelligence tests are less unreliable instruments of selection for future academic work than are tests of attainment, or interviews, and their omission makes selection less accurate.

A much criticized feature of the eleven-plus has been the anxiety created in children by having to sit a formal examination. To avoid this, several authorities now prefer to give a series of tests at intervals in the final year. With the same end in view, the West Riding of Yorkshire adopted in parts of the county the 'Thorne scheme', which provisionally allots a certain number of grammar-school places to each of the junior schools of the area, according to the school's record of eleven-plus successes in the past. In any one year the junior school submits its list of children in its own estimated order of merit. Only the borderline children are then externally assessed, by means of interviews and tests in English and arithmetic. In the light of these assessments the number of grammar-school places given to each junior school is eventually settled. The scheme has the defects of its virtues. On the one hand, most children are untroubled by any formal examination. On the other hand, for those near the borderline too much depends on the accuracy of the junior school's order of merit and on the interview.

One must conclude therefore, that none of the modifications introduced in attempts to meet both popular and expert criticism of the full eleven-plus procedure has been satisfactory. Most people would say: 'If we must have selection at eleven, let it be as fair and accurate as possible.' Intelligence tests, attainment tests in English and mathematics, and junior school records are all necessary, if selection is not to become even less accurate than at present. The mental testers themselves hold out no hope that it will improve significantly. Is this good enough?

The result of all this immensely honest effort by educational psychologists, teachers, and administrators is this: that out of every twenty children picked for the grammar school, six or seven turn out to be unsuited to that type of education, and they keep out another six or seven of the remaining eighty sent to 'modern' schools, who should have been admitted.[1] The true picture may be worse, for it is reasonable to suppose that other 'modern' school children, discouraged by rejection (as they see it), fail to respond there as they might have done had they been allowed to proceed to a grammar school. I recall the case of a boy who scored 109 and 112 in intelligence tests before he failed the eleven-plus examination, and 113 soon afterwards. He was then admitted to a grammar school by a special arrangement; and six weeks after the third test already mentioned, a now confident boy recorded a score of 134.[2] Success breeds success, and failure breeds failure.

If we are to help our children effectively, we certainly must assess their various qualities, measure and appraise them. Tests of various kinds are valuable and necessary for this purpose. Indeed, we need more guidance which is scientifically informed. But such information must be used to advance the progress of all children on a broad and varied front: the open road to personal fulfilment. Instead we have hitherto used it as a regulator, a turnstile through which people are allowed to pass only in single file on production of standardized credentials.

1. cf. Yates and Pidgeon, *Admission to Grammar Schools* (Newnes, 1957) and *15 to 18* (Crowther report), vol. I (H.M.S.O., 1959). p. 72.

2. *British Journal of Educational Psychology*, vol. XXIII, part III, November 1953, p. 151.

The Crowther Report found that twenty-two per cent of Army recruits to national service, and no fewer than twenty-nine per cent of R.A.F. recruits, had had the wrong type of schooling. No observer could find such figures less than gravely disturbing. Is there not, he must ask, some satisfactory alternative which could dispense altogether with selection and segregation at eleven-plus?

The comprehensive school

Between the ages of five and eleven all children, other than the educationally subnormal, the physically handicapped, and those whose parents pay fees for them at independent or direct-grant schools, attend the local primary schools (infant stage 5–7; junior stage 7–11). These primary schools are comprehensive – that is, they take practically all local children, whatever their abilities, and try to give them the education best suited to each individual pupil.

This means a common curriculum for the most part, but of course the subject-matter and the way it is presented are varied to meet the need not only of different classes but of individuals within each class. One school may prefer to have all the clever children together in one class and all the backward children in another, believing that such an arrangement will avoid frustration and facilitate the progress of both sets. Another school may hold that grading children in this way – as A, B, C, or D – damages the self-confidence of those labelled as inferior, and inhibits their future progress. The latter school will have children of widely varying ability in each class. It is therefore more likely to rely on methods which require individual teaching and learning, rather than on the more orthodox practice of teaching the whole class about the same thing and carrying the work on at the same pace for everyone.

Whichever approach is favoured, it is mainly a professional question of the best way of achieving an agreed end – the full development and progress of the individual child. Each of these primary schools is still a comprehensive school.

The comprehensive secondary school is simply an extension of the comprehensive primary school, and has the same aims. It takes practically all the children from a given district between eleven and fifteen or sixteen and – where there is no separate comprehensive college provision beyond sixteen – those who wish to stay on at school till eighteen or nineteen. Because special interests develop as people grow up, such a school must offer a wide range of courses to meet the different needs of different pupils. It may arrange the grouping of children in their classes according to age, general ability, special abilities, special interests, or a combination of some or all of these. This matter, as in the primary school, is mainly a professional one concerning the most effective way of achieving an aim about which there is no disagreement – the full development and progress of the individual pupil.

Such a school will not however be divided into distinct, separately organized sides, such as grammar, technical, and 'modern'. A secondary school so arranged would be a multilateral school, just as a school with two distinct sides (e.g. grammar/technical, technical/'modern', grammar/ 'modern') is a bilateral school. Multilateral and bilateral schools are uneasy compromises between the comprehensive idea and the belief that there should be distinct types of secondary school to cater for different types of child. The terms 'multilateral' and 'bilateral' are now falling into disuse, and no longer appear in the official Statistics of Education.

In January 1968 there were in England and Wales 748 schools officially described as comprehensive. These numbers compare with more than 4,800 secondary schools giving a special type of education – 'modern', technical, or grammar. The comprehensives provided for about 606,000 children (with some 23,000 teachers); the traditional schools of separate type had some 2,225,000 children and 123,000 teachers. The proportion of children who in future will attend schools of comprehensive type is, of course, rising as local authorities' plans for introducing more of them mature. It is officially estimated that the number of comprehensive schools in England and Wales will have risen (in round figures) to about 880 in January 1969, 975 in 1970, and 1,180 in 1971.

No official estimate is available of the proportion of children of secondary school age who will be in comprehensive schools in each of those years – but there is clearly a long way to go before this amounts even to a simple majority.

Can we have quality with equality?

I have said that the English do not believe in equality. This is not because they are innately more snobbish or less capable of idealism than the logical French of the eighteenth century, or than the socialist Russians or democratic Americans of the twentieth. England's role in history has for so long been that of a superior nation and big brother, her people have for so long taken personal and political freedom for granted, that they are not immediately concerned with basic needs, with the upward striving of the oppressed. If 'we've never had it so good' as during the election of 1959, we have always had it pretty good compared with other countries; and so we have become less concerned with basic equality than might otherwise have been the case. With lofty superiority we have looked beyond it, searching rather for quality, and assuming that we cannot have both together.

The average Englishman is confused about the meaning and implications of equality. He takes it for granted that equality implies flat uniformity, that equality in education would impose the same subjects, the same teaching methods, the same pace of progress, on pupils who obviously differ enormously in their ability, interests, and characters.

Though some levelling-up is certainly involved, a featureless levelling-out would of course be a denial of all we have learnt from psychology and education. The differences between individuals are infinitely variable and complex; and our aim is the full development of everyone's talents.

In our consideration of the eleven-plus examination, however, we have noticed some of the difficulties met in attempting to measure these differences, to weigh, assess, *and relate them one to another* in a comparative order of overall merit. It is difficult enough to rank people in relation to one quite specific field of activity: for example, to compare two footballers, one of whom has speed and a strong shot but lacks ball control, the other slow but accurate in passing, with good ball control; or two historians, one meticulous, careful, dry-as-dust; the other imaginative, readable, and too romantic. Really accurate comparative ratings can only be made in relation to a strictly limited subject (and only then in relation to present performance, for we cannot tell how each will develop in the future) – for example, the relative speed with which six men can run 100 yards. The difficulties of judgement multiply if we broaden the field, asking less precisely 'How do they compare as runners?' (various distances being implied) or even more broadly and vaguely 'How do they compare as athletes?'

If the problems of comparative ranking are so great within one field, whether it be athletics or art or housecraft or engineering or languages, how much more difficult it is to arrive at fair overall assessments covering still wider fields! Yet we have presumed to do just this with children at the tender age of eleven. For here we are in fact trying not only to assess their natural aptitudes for different subjects, but also to allow for all the complex influences of environment and personality which have gone to make up the child as he is at this moment of judgement. In our present state of ignorance about the human mind and the springs of behaviour, it is insufferable arrogance not merely to predict at that early point how a person is likely to develop, but to direct him willy-nilly to one course of development rather than another.

The fact that 'modern' schools on the whole offer much poorer opportunities than grammar schools has sharpened this sense of injustice and made it obvious to all. The root failing, however, has lain not in the fact that one type of school is superior to the other, but in the belief that at eleven children can and should be sorted into this type or that and educated accordingly. Attempts to improve the staff and courses of 'modern' schools did not remedy, but only tended to hide this basic flaw in our thinking about and organization of secondary education. The idea that there were two or three types of child, suitable for two or three types of schools, was incredibly crude and naïve.

No two children are the same; that is a truism. The more closely we think about its implications, however, the more we realize that attempts to compare them in general orders of merit are hopelessly unscientific.

The concept of equality in education, therefore, is in fact entirely opposite to the notion of sameness and uniformity, of turning out all children to one pattern. It is rather the concept of equal *worth*, that is, all equally deserving and needing such aids to personal growth as we can give.

In gradually replacing birth and wealth by the ability to pass examinations, we are doing no more than replace one rule for the queueing order by another. Our philosophy is still dominated by the belief that life is a race for a few limited prizes. It is fundamentally a philosophy of limitation and restriction. Its doctrines are that the weakest must go to the wall, that the race is always to the swift and the battle to the strong. It is the bitter, cynical conclusion of the materialist.

Most of us have turned from its crudest manifestations – racial discrimination against colour and the Jews. We have half-turned against its less obvious marks – for example, the social snobberies of schooling and speech. But basically this philosophy is rooted in the idea that one can only advance at the expense of someone else, in relation to that person's failure to keep pace. It is still the law of the jungle.

Against this it is imperative that we repeat *and re-state in modern terms*, applying it in detailed argument each to our own field, the philosophy which, though to Christendom 2,000 years old, is still very new in terms of the whole span of human life on the earth. It is possible for *all* children, *all* adults, to have life and to have it abundantly; but not until we abandon our practice of appropriating the cream to a few and leaving the rest to get what nourishment they can from the blue milk.

America and Russia: a comparison

One does not need to be a selfless idealist in order to appreciate the weakness of recent English thinking on education. From a materialist point of view, the deeply pessimistic belief in a limited pool of ability has caused us rapidly to fall behind in the march of progress. It is a belief rejected by the two leading civilizations of today, though they respond to this situation in different ways, neither of which is fully acceptable to the English people as a whole.

In North America – both U.S.A. and Canada – the common school is an obvious and necessary part of a democratic society. The secondary age range is from twelve to eighteen, as in Scotland. Schools vary from under a hundred pupils to several thousands in size. The former exist because they serve remote settlements as the community's only school, and inevitably offer little more than elementary education. Their number, however, is steadily declining, and they do not adequately represent the character of the normal North American high school.

Specialization in America has brought enlargement of the number of pupils, so that a school of 2,000 to 5,000 is not remarkable, with corresponding enlargement of staff, in total much more variously qualified, and enlargement of curriculum, so that different kinds of ability are all catered for.

The large American high school is no longer primarily a part of the local community, but a self-sufficient community on its own. The staff are fully absorbed in their important, ever-changing, and always demanding work. Not only are there departments staffed by specialists for all the normal subjects; there is also a guidance department run by qualified psychologists whose jobs it is to assess the personality and ability of each pupil and to help him to choose both the right path through school, with its multitude of options, and the right career on leaving school.

It would be wrong to suggest that these large busy schools do not look outwards. They do: but their vision necessarily ranges afar, over the whole American society in which their pupils move, and indeed beyond. As man's mobility increases, so will this trend in education. I do not believe, however, that intimate membership of a local community need obscure the wider view.

Although the Americans have more faith in specialist, especially psychological, guidance than the English, they also have more respect for parents' wishes. Home-and-school associations flourish, and are taken for granted more than parent-teacher associations in England.

The great educational debate in North America, however, is not about the common high school, or its size, or parents' wishes, or the need for a varied curriculum, or the place of psychological guidance. It is about the grouping of children *within* the common school. At present there is little more than the occasional attempt to put the clever children in one class or stream, the average in a second, the slow in a third, and so on. This is partly because of the great influence that American parents have on what happens to their children inside the school. Segregation of a minority of the bright children would imply rejection for the majority; and few parents would willingly accept this. In general it is 'academic', often university intellectuals, who demand more selection and segregation.[1] Professional educationists on the whole resist this demand.

The American's abhorrence of imposed uniformity nevertheless permits great differences in school achievement, not only between one pupil and another, but in the study by any pupil of one subject rather than another. Within a broad curriculum, there is room for much individual choice. Rapid progress in a favourite subject can take a pupil into a class one or two grades higher for that subject, while he pursues others at a more normal pace. The result is a good deal of uneven performance: high-quality work in a few subjects, often mediocre work in the majority. Opportunity to be unequal applies not only to a whole society, but to the education of each individual.

In the Soviet Union a different social philosophy stresses

1. cf. Hilda Neatby, *So Little for the Mind* (Clarke & Urwin, 1953); Jacques Barzun, *The House of Intellect* (Secker & Warburg, 1960); J. D. Koemer, *The Miseducation of American Teachers* (Penguin, Baltimore, 1965).

the importance of equality; not only equality between different people, but the equal importance of subjects in any pupil's curriculum. There is no 'streaming': all classes are of mixed ability. The teacher will strive to take all the pupils forward together as a class in all the subjects. The work will be so organized that slow learners are helped by the quick, working in pairs or in groups. Each pupil is expected to put extra effort, not so much into his good subjects as into his weak ones.

Here, indeed, is the nub of the whole difference between the approach of the American and Soviet societies to education. The latter aims to lift the standard of knowledge and life of all its citizens. It believes that from a uniformly good standard will spring the great performance and the advancement of new learning. The ground will be more fertile. Society will be well informed, educated to understand and react appropriately to the inspiration of each genius it throws up.

America, on the other hand, fears the effect of marshalling minds in standard array. It believes that the great contributions to human life have come from individuals who were allowed or were determined to assert their unique viewpoint, often flatly against the most weighty orthodox opinion. Copernicus, Martin Luther, Charles Darwin, and beyond them Jesus of Nazareth – theirs is the spirit that inspires the thought and works of America's educators, from Dewey to Conant. In short, America believes that the individual comes first, and that society is important chiefly as an environment necessary to the full life of individuals. Russia, aiming no less at achieving human happiness, regards a harmonious and efficient society as a first essential for individual fulfilment; and further assumes that individual satisfaction can best be found by serving society and subordinating one's personal desires to it.

The differences of aim are quite fine, and both have a

more than tenuous link with Christian teaching. The real differences lie in the realm not so much of philosophy as of psychology. A major issue in life is the extent to which we, individuals and societies alike, can grow to maturity. That means how far we can move from helpless dependence to easy, confident independence.

Few complete that journey. Some always retain traces of brash adolescence, the deliberate rejection of orderly living, and the assertion of individual quirks of personal likes, dislikes, and prejudices. Others live for ever under the shadow of authority. In infancy they need it. In adolescence they reject it. Where neither of these earlier stages has been completely and unhurriedly lived through, they grasp again at authority, but this time exercising it, as the easy solution. It is well known that the bullied becomes the bully. Almost every fag longs for the day when his role will be reversed. Adolescent America, authoritarian Russia, are both societies which mirror incomplete human development in different forms. Can an older, more mature social order reconcile the admirable aims of these two mutually uncomprehending young giants? Can we in England show them, in fact, a way through the wood?

Despite all the platitudes of politicians, too few realize how vital is education to the well-being of individuals and society. Yet its aim goes to the heart of all philosophy, to the inner purpose of all government.

I often say to parents: 'What do you want most of all for your children?' Almost invariably they reply: 'I want them to be happy.' Happiness essentially comes with controlled but unperverted growth. It is not to be confused with soft and pleasant living. It implies, in Aristotle's sense, being usefully active, developing according to the laws of one's nature, developing the best in one's nature. Full growth demands exertion, stern testing, adaptation to the environment. Our aim as educators must be the full development of everyone's powers, schooled (because man is a social animal) for use in harmony with those of his fellows. Our pupils are like the tall young trees in the plantation, which grow up straight and strong towards the light precisely because they are in the close company of others.

We need, first, a culturally rich environment of home, school and neighbourhood, within which children can learn and grow. We need a frank recognition that individuals are unique, their differences immensely (indeed immeasurably) varied, and demanding great flexibility of both teachers and administrators. We need to weld three outstanding features from the societies we have mentioned: the Soviet insistence on raising the educational level of all, rather than allowing a few fast starters to monopolize the field; America's concern for the freedom of the individual to move at his own best pace, along the lines he needs; England's traditional faith that only the highest standards of teaching and learning are acceptable – not merely to others, but above all to oneself. Fundamentally such a programme is a call for quality geared to the needs of a liberal, democratic society.

Can it be done? In particular, how far does the English comprehensive school succeed in its attempt to provide the answer?

2. Framework

1. EVOLUTION

WHEN, by a curious stroke of fortune, at the age of fourteen I was translated from my village elementary school to the ancient grammar school ten miles away, I entered a different world. For the first time I wore a tailored grey suit, stiff collar, and school cap. I felt a guilty turncoat when the elementary-school children of the town chanted 'Grammar, grammar matchstalks' derisively at us as we walked long-trousered through the cobbled streets.

Inside the school, too, my life was turned upside down. It was not only that for the first time I encountered such subjects as Latin and French, physics and chemistry, algebra and geometry; I had expected that. What amazed me was the elaborate apparatus devised to get boys to do what the staff wanted. Essays and tests all reaped their quota of marks, religiously added up and announced at half term and end of term. There were colours for doing well at rugger and cricket; points for one's house, prizes for this, lines or even the cane for that ... I was surprised, because none of this was known in my little village school, where we worked (and at the appropriate times played) because after all wasn't that what we went to school for? I was more than surprised, I was bewildered, because despite this host of incentives, most of the grammar-school pupils were more reluctant to do their best than any of my fellows in the village. Yet for classroom competence, devotion to their job, and interest in their pupils' progress, the grammar school staff could not have been bettered. It was the system that was different.

I had still to learn that there was yet a third world of 'public' schools operating on a level as remote from the grammar school as the latter was from the elementary school. The grammar school's strangely formal rituals were in fact copied from the 'public' school Olympians. Its best features – the teachers' deep interest in and concern for every pupil, complemented by the town's pride in its little, ancient school – sprang from the school's roots in the local community.

Up to 1944 three distinct systems of education existed in England. There were elementary, secondary, and independent schools. Local education authorities and voluntary bodies such as the churches, supported by grants from the government's Board of Education, provided free, compulsory, basic education from five to fourteen in elementary schools.

Secondary education was a superior type of education given partly in grammar schools of old foundation and partly in schools established and run by local authorities. Fees were normally charged, but some free places were given to elementary-school children who won scholarships in the examinations held around the age of eleven. The number of such free places varied widely from one district to another, but over the whole country worked out around fourteen per cent in 1944. The Labour-dominated Durham County Council ensured that every place in its secondary schools went to children who qualified in the eleven-plus scholarship examination. This 100 per cent free-place system replaced parents' wealth by pupils' ability as the criterion for admission, and anticipated the post-1944 eleven-plus examination.

Apart from the secondary schools provided or aided by local authorities, there were other schools which were either completely independent of state aid and control, or which accepted money and inspection direct from the central government ('direct grant') but not from local authorities. Many of the former were poor and far from efficient, some downright disreputable; but all gained something in the eyes of a status-seeking public from the glamour of the great independent schools. Most of these were boys' boarding schools, which were not only well endowed but whose reputation enabled them to charge high fees. Eton, Harrow, Winchester, Charterhouse, Rugby ... these and some seventy more were the schools which dominated the corridors of power. Their old pupils ran the empire, monopolized the seats in Conservative Cabinets, controlled the Foreign Office, the Treasury, the Civil Service, and the City. It was a common aim of self-made men to get their sons into such schools and ensure their future acceptance by people who mattered.

A fairly high standard of entry was demanded of candidates whose families had no longstanding connexion with such schools. Other applicants, like the young Winston Churchill many years before, found the formal examination no serious barrier. But the 'public' schools, as the most famous independent schools were confusingly called, should not be blamed for this. Their function was to educate the children of the ruling class and train them to lead. A well-known Oxford don was once heard to observe: 'Whatever the movement, good or bad, it will be led by an Etonian.' Birth and wealth still counted. The rise of the meritocracy, though imminent, had not yet begun to shape a new social order. Each 'public' school had its traditions and its special religious or educational emphasis which old pupils wanted their own children to experience. The continuity and security which the schools derived from such support was not only economic. The boarding school, being detached from the local community, needs in its place other, stable, human ties.

Nevertheless the 'public' schools were becoming anomalies in a society which, under the pressure of war, was moving rapidly towards democracy. Many of their heads and old pupils were aware of this, and in 1944 the Fleming Report recommended that they should accept twenty-five per cent of their pupils from the State system. The recommendation was not implemented, for it was a compromise appealing to few, and attacked by many for quite different reasons. Local authorities did not relish the prospect of losing the better pupils from their own schools and paying high fees to boot. Radical reformers disliked the idea of bolstering schools for the rich by the infusion of talent from below, and suspected that selected working-class children would be indoctrinated with upper-class attitudes. Rigid conservatives, on the other hand, feared that the special character of the 'public' school would be completely destroyed if the basis of entry were to be so largely changed.

All these points in fact are valid. The proposal, though with the proportion of State pupils boosted to fifty per cent, has been revived in the 1968 report of the Public Schools Commission – and it commands as little popularity as ever.

In 1944, then, there were the three types of school: elementary for the working class, secondary for the middle class (to join which schools one working-class child in seven might aspire), 'public' or independent for the upper class. The injustice shouted aloud to a people who were, as it was the fashion for Conservative politicians to observe, 'all socialists now'; a strangely idealistic people, who in orthodox rural Skipton could choose a radical Common Wealth supporter of Richard Acland as their Member of Parliament. Such was the new force which brought into existence, with all-party approval, a great Education Act.

The 1944 Education Act

This Act made many notable decisions, not all of which have yet been implemented. The one which caught public

imagination and won everyone's approval, yet whose application has aroused the most bitter controversy, was the
introduction of 'secondary education for all'. In future
the elementary and secondary schools were to be fused into one system, itself then re-divided into two *stages*: the
first ('primary') for children up to the age of twelve, and a
second ('secondary') to which all children would go – com-
pulsorily to fifteen, and beyond that age if they wished.
Eventually, at some unspecified date, the minimum leaving
age was to be raised to sixteen.

It is true that independent schools were still left outside, apart from being subjected to inspection and approval
by the Ministry of Education;[1] but it was felt important
not to impose uniformity. If the State schools were
brought up to the best standards, it would no longer be
possible for rich people to buy better material conditions
by paying high fees to independent schools. The latter's
justification would lie in their special characteristics – the
Quaker schools' stress on religion and toleration, the Anglican atmosphere of Lancing or Marlborough, the unorthodox manliness of Abbotsholme and Gordonstoun, or
A. S. Neill's revolutionary practice of love and freedom at
Summerhill. It would have been a great loss to the bur-
geoning power of educational thought and practice had any
such schools been either closed or brought under local control.

Within the State system, schools were to be maintained
or aided by local education authorities, the county and
county-borough councils, under the 'control and direction'
of a Minister of Education. The Act said that it was the duty
of these authorities to provide primary education for children up to twelve and secondary education for children aged

1. Renamed 'Department of Education and Science', under a
Secretary of State, in 1964.

twelve and over (later, permissively, ten years six months and over). The schools which were to provide this secondary education were to be 'sufficient in number, character, and equipment to afford for all pupils ... such variety of instruction and training as may be desirable in view of their different ages, abilities, and aptitudes, and of the different periods for which they may be expected to remain at school'.

Exception to this principle has never been taken. It is over the interpretation of the sentence that the fiercest public battle in England's educational history has been waged.

It might be thought that the obvious meaning was that just as a sufficient number of well-equipped primary schools is required to meet the very different needs of all the local children who go there, so each secondary school must have a full range of courses, staff, and equipment to serve the developing needs of these same children in due course whether they stay at school beyond fifteen or not. In the same way, most independent schools take pupils with a wide range of ability and aptitude. They too need to make very varied provision for a great diversity of talent.

But the officials of the Ministry of Education, and of most of the local education authorities, did not think in this way. Indeed, the outlook of most professional educators – teachers and administrators alike – had for a generation taken on a new slant under the influence of a school of educational psychologists whose prime concern was mental measurement.

The leading figure in this movement was Dr Cyril Burt. In 1926 he had assured the Hadow Committee that it was possible by means of intelligence tests to make a fairly accurate assessment of a child's mental capacity by the age of twelve. Burt and his followers not only thought heredity mattered far more than environment in determining mental ability, but believed they could distinguish inborn ability well enough for practical purposes. These practical purposes were the separation of clever from average children, average from dull, either in separate classes or in separate schools.

This belief in both the immediate validity and the long-term stability of intelligence testing led the Spens Committee in 1938 to recommend the establishment of three main types of school (academic, technical, and general) for children of different aptitudes and different levels of ability. The doctrine was reaffirmed in a less subtle way in the Norwood report of 1943. Its influence was clearly dominant in the White Paper which preceded the 1944 Act. The White Paper proposed that secondary education should be organized in three main types of secondary school; and though that proposal was not specifically included in the Act, the Ministry's officials were not, as we shall see, to be deterred from getting their own way in practice.

Labour Government, 1945–51

Before the issue could be brought to a head, the war-time coalition had been replaced in 1945 by a Labour government pledged to social reform. One might have supposed that an avowedly socialist party would look askance at plans for separate types of secondary school which offered courses of different length and scope to children judged superior or inferior in mental ability: schools which were, therefore, likely to vary greatly in social prestige.

But Labour was not an egalitarian party, though it included some egalitarians in its ranks. Although it had then, as now, several teacher M.P.s and the sympathy of many professors and administrators, few of the leading figures had the knowledge which would have enabled them effectively to answer the arguments of Ministry officials. Still more important, most saw no need to do so.

Much of Labour's thinking was a generation out of date. Here was a party too long starved of office, deeply concerned to make changes that were overdue. But sometimes a changed situation and new knowledge make the once-sought improvement itself inadequate. Time has overtaken it. So it was with education. Labour's general attitude here is epitomized by the attitude of the traditionally Labour Durham County Council. When secondary education had been available only to a minority, Durham had been in the van in building its own secondary schools and accepting only 'scholarship' boys and girls. Brains had rightly been preferred to wealth and birth. The bright poor boy, in the best reforming tradition, was given his chance.

The trouble was that the good party men of Durham and elsewhere were so drunk with the virtue of this advance that they failed to see it was but a step on the way. All living things change. No form of social institution can expect to do more than serve its turn usefully, before yielding place to new.

It was, then, under the nominal direction of two sincere but ill-equipped Labour ministers – first Ellen Wilkinson, then George Tomlinson – that Ministry officials took steps to ensure that their preference for a divided form of secondary education should prevail. The first of a series of Ministry pamphlets (*The Nation's Schools*, 1945) assumed that the development plans then being prepared by local authorities would be based on three types of secondary school. It offended progressive opinion, and was withdrawn; but a circular of December 1945, giving 'guidance' to local authorities on the establishment of secondary schools, proceeded on much the same assumption.

Even so, some local education authorities, notably London, Middlesex, Coventry, Oldham, and the West Riding, decided to provide comprehensive secondary schools. They were to be sufficiently large, well staffed, and equipped to meet the needs of all the pupils of the district who required full-time schooling between the ages of eleven and nineteen. The West Riding's development plan, issued in 1948, said:

The Committee ... have been unable to accept certain suggestions which have been made or implied in various reports or Ministerial circulars. They cannot, for instance, agree that at the age of eleven children can be classified into three recognized mental types, and should be allocated to grammar, modern, and technical schools accordingly;

that the numbers to go to each type of school should be determined by an arbitrary percentage of the age group;

or

that at the age of eleven children show certain aptitudes which can be relied upon to indicate the type of secondary school to which a child should be allocated.[1]

But the majority of local authorities – whether from principle, convenience, or apathy – took the other route. Former secondary schools were re-named grammar schools, to which only children successful in an examination at or before the age of eleven were admitted. Some authorities converted old 'junior technicals' into technical secondary schools, to take the next layer of ability. Senior elementary schools of pre-war days, labelled, ungrammatically, 'secondary modern' schools, were left to go on much as before.

The latter was much the easier course. Grammar-school teachers were often a little fearful of being called on to teach difficult and backward boys and girls. They had had dull pupils before the war, it is true, but they were usually the docile dull from respectable fee-paying families. They

1. *Education*, 15 October 1948.

disliked the possibility of losing their hitherto superior status in the town. They thought that school standards in scholarship and behaviour would suffer if the doors were flung open to all. Many had little or no understanding of the interests and needs of non-academic pupils, and felt honestly that such pupils would be better taught by those who had.

Conversely, the non-graduate heads and staff of the former elementary schools were apprehensive about being passed over for graduates in competition for the top jobs in a comprehensive system. Some graduates, too, realizing that their prospects of a headship in a grammar or comprehensive school were nil, chose to carve a niche for themselves in the 'secondary moderns'. But these were motives rarely voiced in public debate. The theory justifying the system was put out in 1947 in a notable Ministry of Education pamphlet, *The New Secondary Education*.

Even at the time, this pamphlet seemed remarkably naïve. Children suitable for a grammar school, dreamed the authors, 'are attracted by the abstract approach to learning'. 'Some children, on the other hand, will have decided at quite an early stage to make their careers in branches of industry or agriculture ... Others may need a course ... with a particular emphasis on commercial subjects or art. All these boys and girls will find their best outlet in the secondary technical school.' This statement, implying that a child's future path should be determined by his childish preferences at eleven, finds no support whatever in educational research. Moreover, the selection procedures devised before or since 1947 made no serious attempt to detect special aptitudes for different kinds of job. Instead, selection was based on all-round ability. The technical school merely got the children who failed to qualify for the grammar school, without regard to their suitability for technical education.

'The majority', says the pamphlet, 'will do best in a

school which provides a good all-round education in an atmosphere which enables them to develop freely along their own lines.' One cannot think of a better aim for the education of the minority either. Unfortunately the reality in 'secondary modern' schools was, and is, a grotesque distortion of this ideal. The initial stamp of failure on all incoming pupils; the large classes compared with those of selective and independent schools; an inequitable Burnham Scale diverting most special-responsibility payments to selective schools, with their bigger proportion of older pupils – all these have militated against the creation of an atmosphere in which different individual needs could be met.

A lukewarm argument for comprehensive schools was presented, but it was assumed that such schools must be very large, with at least 1,500 pupils. Since nearly all secondary schools then catered for fewer than 600 children it was clear that, if this assumption were correct, comprehensive schools must be few and far between and would have to be specially built. The case for a two-tier end-on comprehensive system, though propounded as early as 1944,[1] was not mentioned; yet it offered the one practical alternative to the tripartite system, since only by that means could all existing schools be brought economically and efficiently into a comprehensive pattern.

The hard facts which determined the attitude of the administrators were twofold. First, the theoretical pattern fitted the picture of pre-war grammar schools, junior technical schools, and senior elementary schools like a glove: it was so convenient. Secondly, the leading administrators were in general committed to segregationist practice and were reluctant to entertain the possibility that they were wrong. Widespread reform began to gather way as they were replaced by new and uncommitted men.

1. e.g. in *The Times Educational Supplement*, 9 September 1944, R. Pedley, 'Reform in Higher Education'.

Fundamentally, secondary school organization at this vital period (1945–51) was befogged and bedevilled by the tremendous hold on almost all educationists which the movement for intelligence testing had acquired. It would be wrong to blame Ministry and local officials too harshly for following the generally accepted evidence of the 'experts' at that time. Where comprehensive schools were planned, it was either in rural areas like the Isle of Man and Anglesey, for simple reasons of economy and efficiency, or in socialist strongholds like London and Coventry, for social-educational reasons. In general, so long as people believed that selection was being made accurately and that children's further performance could be fairly foretold by the tests in use, they were unconcerned. The destruction of the inflated claims of the intelligence testers, which was to change the whole picture, was still to come.

One highly significant feature of the political and social scene in post-war Britain, however, is spotlighted by the curious attitude of different sections of the Labour party to the question of the eleven-plus, and to the comprehensive school, throughout the period from 1944 to the present day. Whether selection could be made accurately or not, the arguments in favour of building classless yet richly diversified local communities round common schools were powerful. They were indeed an accepted part of socialist thought. Grouping by ability within these schools could still take place if desired. The alternative – forced segregation of children in separate schools, with the awful implications of daily, publicly, hammering home a child's officially assessed inferiority – should surely have been anathema to Labour. Yet, as we have seen, a Labour government, with massive electoral backing for social reform, chose the segregationist course.

London, fired by the informed vision of people like

Margaret Cole and Harold Shearman, showed in its plan for comprehensive secondary education how the enormous difficulties might be overcome. A few other authorities planned likewise. But the implementation of all these plans was delayed for years by economic troubles; and in Staffordshire, Middlesex, and the West Riding, changes in political control also meant changes in plans for secondary education before much of significance could be done.

Conservative Government, 1951–64

Even so, there were counties and county boroughs which from 1945 had undisturbed Labour majorities for at least twenty years. They were:[1]

County Councils	County Borough Councils	
Derbyshire	Barnsley	Rotherham
Durham	Barrow-in-Furness	St Helens
Glamorgan	Blackburn	Salford
London	Burnley	Sheffield
Monmouthshire	Coventry	Stoke-on-Trent
Nottinghamshire	Derby	Sunderland
	Gateshead (since 1946)	Swansea
		Wakefield
	Kingston-upon-Hull	Warrington
	Merthyr Tydfil	West Ham
	Middlesbrough	Wigan
	Norwich	

For twenty years most of these authorities did little or nothing to apply the principles of the party to which they nominally subscribed. They pleaded that Conservative governments did all in their power to prevent or restrict a changeover to comprehensive secondary education.

There is some truth in this. If Labour was timid, Conservative resistance was stupidly obstructionist. In 1954, a major storm broke when the Minister of Education, Miss

1. I am indebted to the Labour Party (Transport House) for this information.

Florence Horsbrugh, refused to permit the London County Council to close Eltham Hill Girls' Grammar School and transfer these 'selected' pupils to its first big new new comprehensive school, Kidbrooke. Miss Horsbrugh also refused to allow the L.C.C. to expand the Bec Boys' Grammar School into a comprehensive school.

In the following year Miss Horsbrugh's successor, Sir David Eccles, forced the proud city of Manchester to its knees. Manchester had proposed the development of three comprehensive schools in the Wythenshawe area. Assuming that the Minister's approval would be forthcoming, it had gone ahead with its plans, and proposed to open these schools in September 1955; but the assumption was unjustified. The Minister refused to sanction two of the schools, which were new foundations, although the comprehensive development of an existing secondary school, Yew Tree, was allowed to proceed. Faced with the threatened loss of grant for the upkeep of the new schools, Manchester was forced to climb down.

Thereafter, Conservative Ministers made it clear that while they were prepared to sanction the development of comprehensive schools in rural areas and on new housing estates, they would not allow their development if it would mean the abolition of an existing efficient grammar school.

The fact is, however, that the Minister of Education did not have unlimited powers of control. His approval was only required for the closing of an existing school, the opening of a new one, or the enlargement of an existing school to such a degree that it amounted in practice to a new one. If no substantial changes in building were involved, a local education authority was free to change the character of a school as it wished, without consulting the Minister at all. Sir David Eccles made this perfectly clear in the Wythenshawe dispute when he made no attempt to restrict the comprehensive development of Yew Tree

School. Lord Hailsham and Sir Edward Boyle reiterated this principle in 1957, when Leicestershire in effect changed some of its 'modern' and grammar schools into junior and senior comprehensive schools respectively.[1]

Clearly, therefore, it was open to any local education authority to tackle the real problem, the organization of its *existing* schools, in a different way. One cannot resist the conclusion that, although the myth of fair and accurate selection had been exposed since the middle fifties, at least a score of inactive Labour authorities did not want to change. Living on the memory of past deeds and ambitions, their character was essentially conservative. The wind of radical thought and reforming zeal chilled their old bones. I began by saying that England is an aristocratic not a democratic society. It seems that many local Labour party leaders have been content that this should be so.

But while Labour was either apathetic or frustrated, a development of great significance was taking place in a Conservative county : Leicestershire.

Drawbacks of the 11–18 school

During the early 1950s thinking on comprehensive development was heavily coloured by London experience and attitudes. It was assumed that a comprehensive school, like a grammar school, must have a sixth form taking pupils up to the age of eighteen; and because the proportion who could be expected to stay at school to that point was then small, it followed that a sixth form large enough to offer a wide range of courses without extravagant use of staff could only be produced from a very large comprehensive school. This London image of the outsize comprehensive school, successful enough in the crowded metropolis, was

1. On the constitutional implications, cf. *Journal of Education*, January 1958, pp. 4–5 : R. Pedley, 'Lord Hailsham's Legacy'.

used as a scarecrow by the supporters of selection. Many Labour politicians, with the notable exception of Alice Bacon, clung to it unimaginatively; yet it was obvious that early and widespread reform could only come if a more flexible organization of secondary education were introduced.

The argument for a new look ran like this: (1) a comprehensive school needs to have a sixth form of at least 120 pupils if it is to meet modern requirements; (2) on average in the mid-fifties it took a comprehensive school of 1,750 pupils aged eleven to eighteen to produce a sixth form of this size; (3) there are educational objections to such large schools; (4) even if these objections are thought invalid, it is certain that large schools sufficient in number to house all children of secondary age cannot be provided for many, many years – yet the need to reform the segregated school system is urgent.

Let me take these points in turn.

1. A sixth-form class of optimum size numbers perhaps eight to twelve pupils. This ensures reasonable economy in the use of highly-qualified teachers, who are all too scarce. It also promotes educational efficiency; the group is small enough to allow the teacher to attend properly to each pupil, big enough to encourage lively discussion.

A school catering for all sorts and conditions of students should offer twenty subjects or more at advanced level, if it is to do the job properly. Each of the following departments will itself need to provide two, three, or perhaps four subjects: modern languages, classics, science, mathematics, engineering, commercial subjects, housecraft, heavy crafts, and the fine arts. Since the sixth form is a stage of education covering at least two and often three years, a fully developed comprehensive school may expect to have at least fifty sixth-form classes. Each pupil will be a member of perhaps four of these. If the normal size of these classes is around ten pupils, as I have suggested, a sixth form of 120 or more becomes necessary to justify staffing and equipment on a really efficient scale.

It was shown some years ago that schools with large sixth forms did distinctly better *per pupil*, in work for the advanced level of GCE, than schools with small sixth forms.[1] Dr Richard Lynn found, first, that girls' grammar schools in London, with much smaller sixth forms, got only half the distinctions per hundred pupils that the boys' schools did. This could hardly have been due to a different level of intelligence between boys and girls. Secondly, he found that while the large boys' grammar schools got only eight per cent more passes at ordinary level than the smaller boys' grammar schools, at advanced level two years later they got a hundred per cent more distinctions per hundred candidates. This must have been due to superior sixth-form education in the larger schools.

In open scholarships to Oxford and Cambridge this tendency is even more pronounced. Certainly the leading schools in the Oxbridge scholarship-league tables over the years have been such schools as Dulwich (466 in the sixth form: 25 open awards in 1967–8); St Paul's (365:24); Eton (499:23); Winchester (375:20); and Manchester G.S. 528:18).[2]

2. If we could have an average local secondary school the size of whose age-groups was in proportion to the Ministry of Education's aggregated figures for all the maintained secondary schools in England and Wales in 1967, it would need to total 1,875 pupils aged eleven to eighteen in

1. *British Journal of Sociology*, June 1959, pp. 129–36.
2. *The Times Educational Supplement*, 30 August 1968: G. D. N. Worswick, 'Men's Awards at Oxbridge, 1967–8'.

order to produce 120 of that number in the sixth form. Contrast this with a leading independent school such as Rugby, which has a thirteen-to-eighteen age-range, and where about half of the 700 boys do sixth-form work. The picture in recognized independent secondary schools as a whole is similar, as the diagram on page 48 shows.

Numbers at the top of the independent 'public' school justify the provision of well-qualified staff and ample equipment. There is no extravagance, for both are fully used. Yet because the proportion of older pupils is high, total numbers need not be great.

Those comprehensive schools which have been established for some years, however, are keeping at school after fifteen perhaps thirty per cent more pupils than the average for the country as a whole. We may therefore accept that most schools of 1,400 not 1,875 will meet the requirement of 120 in the sixth form. When compulsory schooling is extended to sixteen the picture will be transformed. Comprehensive schools of no more than 1,000 pupils aged eleven to eighteen may reasonably expect to have 120 or more engaged in sixth, seventh, and eighth year courses.

3. The educational objections to very big schools are as follows.

First, they tend to be run on a hierarchical basis. The ordinary class teacher may find himself far removed from the centre of effective discussion and decision. In the small school he counts for a lot, in the big school for much less. Offsetting this, however, he is likely to find a bigger staff more stimulating. Where there are people with a great variety of interests and qualifications, the environment of the staffroom is likely to be rich and diverse, never mean and narrow.

I. ALL L.E.A. SECONDARY SCHOOLS
(England and Wales: January 1967)
1 mm. (horizontal): 10,000 pupils

II. ALL RECOGNIZED INDEPENDENT
SECONDARY SCHOOLS
(England and Wales: January 1967)
1 mm. (horizontal): 200 pupils

Age-groups

Secondly, in a big school the intimacy necessary for the deeprooted growth of a community is much more difficult to achieve. In the small school, whether you happen to teach a child or not, you and he still know each other quite well. Your responsibility for him, his responsibility to you, are taken for granted by both. In the outsize school, to note good or bad behaviour you may need your notebook, like a policeman, to get the boy's name and class. A chit is called for to inform his tutor, if in a busy day it seems worth-while going to those lengths. A hundred yards outside the school, pupil and teacher may each be to the other no more than a vaguely familiar face, the most casual of acquaintances.[1]

A teacher commented to me on his own big school's carol festival: 'As many as 300 children take part; several choirs are involved, soloists, the school orchestra. But one comes to long for smaller numbers on the platform, a more intimate atmosphere, less tramping about of pupils between carols.'

Objections of this kind apply to all big schools, of course, whatever the type. They find expression in stories such as the doubtless apocryphal one of two boys who were taking a scholarship at Oxford: 'Which school do you come from?' 'Manchester Grammar School.' 'So do I.'

Finally, the average child. We need not worry here about the bright, the dull, the delinquent, the unusual of any sort – they always win attention. It is the ordinary boy who needs to feel that he counts – not for anything special that

1. The head of a comprehensive school, Mrs Chetwynd, has given a different view: 'By keeping records on paper and not in our heads, the method suggested as a better alternative, we place our knowledge based on personal contact at the disposal of all other interested colleagues who wish to share our understanding of the child.' (*Comprehensive School*, Routledge and Kegan Paul, 1960, pp. 101–2).

he can do (he often cannot do anything special), but
simply for himself. In spite of the division of big schools
into smaller social units such as houses and tutorial
groups, many fear that he will be overlooked. Comprehensive school teachers certainly try to prevent this, but I
have found them divided on the extent to which they are
successful.

4. The educational objections are very largely matters of
opinion. Some will dismiss them, and they may be right
in doing so. We must nevertheless face the fact that out of
5,576 secondary schools in England and Wales in 1968,
only 265 provided for more than 1,000 pupils; and no
more than 588 schools (including those 265) took more
than 800 pupils. At the other extreme, 1,941 secondary
schools had fewer than 400 pupils.

Many of our schools occupy post-war buildings which
cannot conceivably be scrapped. The capital investment
required to replace them by schools for over 1,000 pupils
would be enormous. New spacious sites would often be
impossible to find. The whole programme would take
many years to implement – too many. If one believes that
segregation at eleven is harmful, such delay in starting the
necessary reforms becomes intolerable. Another solution
must be found.

Two-tier secondary education

There is such an alternative to the very large school. It has
been canvassed in this country ever since 1944 in various
forms, and it has its precedents abroad, particularly in
North America.

Immediately following the 1944 Act it was obvious to
a small minority of people that the drawbacks of selection at eleven on the one hand and huge comprehensive
schools on the other could be resolved – and, moreover,

quickly and economically resolved – by putting existing small and medium-sized schools end-on to provide secondary education in two stages.[1] In 1954 Croydon's education officials made a powerful case for combining all the borough's sixth forms in a 'junior college'. Early proposals for such reform, however, foundered on two rocks: the slightness of statistical evidence against selection at eleven, and the reluctance of grammar-school and comprehensive-school teachers to lose their older pupils to a separate institution.

From about 1953 onwards, however, parents' dissatisfaction with eleven-plus selection began to receive weighty backing from the researches of scholars and from facts given in the official report on *Early Leaving* (1954). This report showed that of the twenty children in every hundred picked for grammar schools at the age of eleven, barely nine reached the normal grammar-school target of five or more passes at the ordinary level of GCE, or an equivalent standard. Indeed, of those who were in the top third of the eleven-plus pass lists, fewer than two out of three were successful by this criterion. On the other hand, late transfers to the grammar school of those who had originally failed at eleven came out slightly better than the whole group of eleven-plus successes.

By the mid-fifties the number of pupils staying longer at school had increased to such an extent that a two-tier system no longer necessarily involved the decapitation of the grammar schools; all but the tiniest could become schools for higher secondary education only. Most 'modern' schools, for their part, had developed well enough to contemplate tackling the early years of secondary education for all pupils.

1. cf. *Education*, 18 and 25 February 1949, R. Pedley, 'County College and Sixth Form', and Labour Party, *Challenge to Britain*, 1953.

This new evidence[1] aroused the interest of administrators at both national and local levels. For example, in May 1955 I was invited to put to the Midland branch of the Association of Education Officers the case for the two-tier system as it might apply in this country. At a meeting with the Minister of Education and senior officials at the Ministry in the following year (1956) I suggested an interim scheme whereby all children should go direct from primary to the existing 'modern' schools, which would thus become junior comprehensive schools, and spend at least three years there. At the age of fourteen, all who wished to go to the grammar schools would do so without examination, provided their parents agreed to keep them there for at least two years. The others would complete their education in the junior comprehensive school.

The advantages of this modified plan were as follows:

1. The secondary schooling of all children who stayed in the converted 'modern' schools would be unbroken.

2. Those going to the grammar school at fourteen would have two years before taking the GCE, like most entrants to 'public' schools.

3. It was likely to be more acceptable to grammar school teachers than would be the transfer of all children at fourteen or fifteen. Though they would have to start coping with a much wider range of ability, at least there was a precedent for that in the pre-war days of fee-payers. Their recruits would at any rate be willing – or at worst would be the unwilling children of willing parents, who could be relied upon to support the school.

4. A promise to keep children at grammar schools for at

1. cf. R. Pedley , 'Comprehensive Education: a non-party solution' (*Schoolmaster*, 8 April 1955), 'The Way Ahead' (*Schoolmaster*, 23 November 1956), and *Comprehensive Education: a new approach* (Gollancz, 1956).

least two years, though it could not be enforced, would ensure that parents did not lightly choose a grammar-school education for one year only, for the sake of status.

In making these proposals I was aware of some obvious deficiencies. The two-year undertaking would have the effect of discouraging poor parents, or those parents, usually working-class, who do not readily see the value of higher education and would not commit themselves for two years ahead. The new style 'grammar school' would be neither a selective school for academic pupils nor a proper senior comprehensive school. It would in fact be much more like the local grammar school of pre-war days, except that ability to pay a modest fee for day pupils would now be replaced by ability and willingness to keep the child longer at school. Again, the creation of a 'rump' of pupils in the last year of the converted 'modern' school did not look like a permanently satisfactory solution. They would be the pupils who had decided that they wished to leave school as soon as possible, and had nothing more to work for, who seemed likely to be the less able and less well-behaved boys and girls, too.

The plan was envisaged only as an interim measure. Its great virtue seemed that it offered a practical way, under existing conditions, of doing away with the eleven-plus examination and enforced segregation of children thereafter. It would be a step on the way to a still better system.

The experiment in Leicestershire

In the following year (1957) Leicestershire decided to adopt in two areas, Wigston and Hinckley, a plan very similar to that described above. The main difference lay in the county's decision to accelerate the progress of very bright children from the primary school to the sixth form by promoting these 'flyers' (roughly eight to ten per cent of a whole age-group) from primary to the new junior high school at the age of ten, and from the junior high school to the senior grammar school at thirteen. By this means, such bright pupils would be able to take GCE (ordinary level) at fifteen and gain an extra year in the sixth form. This early transfer of 'flyers' necessarily involved the movement of some children from primary to secondary education below the legal minimum age of ten years sixth months. It was, however, commonly practised by other local education authorities, and the Ministry turned a blind eye on it.

Later the county was to decide that the early advancement of clever children was unsatisfactory on educational grounds: too many found the social and psychological strain too great, and failed to fulfil their early promise. The practice was therefore discontinued.

The scheme was begun in Leicestershire in a modified way. Free transfer from 'modern' to grammar school at fourteen for all who wished it was introduced at once, and this ensured a welcome from many worried and disappointed parents; but for the first two years at Wigston, and the first three at Hinckley, problems of accommodation made it necessary for the authority to continue to select the top twelve and a half per cent for direct transfer from primary to grammar schools at the age of eleven. When this ceased, so did the eleven-plus examination. Indeed, the reorganized districts of Leicestershire were the first areas in England (not Wales) where the eleven-plus was abolished. All children are now promoted at eleven-plus, none at ten-plus, and spend three years in the converted 'modern' school, now termed 'high school'. At fourteen, after consultation with the teachers, parents decide whether they wish their child to go to the grammar school for at least two more years. If so, they are asked to sign a statement to this effect.

The scheme has now been extended to all parts of the

county, and when the leaving age is raised to sixteen all children will transfer from the high school to the upper school (as the grammar school is now called) at fourteen. Indeed, this has already been anticipated in two high schools, where the number wishing to leave at fifteen is so small that they too go to the upper school at fourteen; and though they are not obliged to stay there more than one year, in fact some do, with good results.

Leicestershire's successful experiment had a big impact on both professional and public opinion, because it demonstrated that an early end to eleven-plus selection was possible everywhere. It was, however, rivalled in importance by another movement, which brought a new force into English educational politics.

In 1960 a group of middle-class parents in Cambridge, including some with university connexions, formed an Association for the Advancement of State Education. They had liberal views on education, disliked the idea of sending their children away from home to 'public' schools, but deplored the tension which a selective system imposed on children and teachers in primary schools whose principles and practice they found otherwise constructive and wholesome. They were concerned, too, about the hazards of selection itself, and about the deficiencies of the secondary schools to which their children might be sent. Unlike the great majority of parents they were well informed about educational issues and articulate in expressing their views.

The influence of this group soon ranged far beyond Cambridge. Other associations were formed in various parts of the country, and when these joined in the Confederation for the Advancement of State Education (CASE) the existing power structure had to take account of it. Pressure on local officials and councillors, on politicians and other public figures, was applied steadily and with growing effect. What happened in schools was no longer left to be settled between 'the office' on the one hand and the teachers on the other; at long last the forgotten people, the parents, were claiming and getting a real say in the kind of education provided for their children. In my view it was these knowledgeable middle-class parents who focused public attention on the problem and built up the necessary national impetus for action. By the time Labour came to power the country was not only willing to accept comprehensive reorganization : it was demanding it.

Labour Government since 1964

In January 1965 Michael Stewart announced that the Government proposed to end selection at eleven and re-organize the schools on the comprehensive principle.

Six months later, in July 1965, his successor at the Department of Education and Science, Anthony Crosland, issued Circular 10/65, which must be one of the most permissive documents ever to be issued from Curzon Street. It requested (it did not order) local education authorities to prepare plans for the reorganization of their secondary schools on comprehensive lines, and to submit them to the Department for approval within twelve months. It also indicated the various patterns which would be found acceptable – and this range was so great as to create misgivings in the minds of some of the firmest advocates of reform.

There is much to be said for flexibility, particularly when one is probing for ways and means of by-passing a system which is obviously an obstacle to progress; and under a government hostile to the comprehensive principle all these various devices had their uses. This does not mean, however, that they are all equally desirable in the climate of opinion which now prevails. At the Labour Party's local government conference of 1964 Mr Crossman, then Labour's chief spokesman on education, emphasized the importance of tidying up the proliferation of plans for secondary education. There is no doubt that had he been at Curzon Street greater attention would have been given to rationalization. On a compact island, with an increasingly mobile population, we cannot afford to have great discrepancies between districts in the organization of our educational system.

On the other hand a remarkable benefit accrued from the loose rein with which Mr Crosland handled the matter. It sparked off a tremendous democratic debate on our schools, and what was to be done about them, throughout the length and breadth of England. Never before can there have been so many public meetings, so many little working parties, so many inches of correspondence columns in the local and national Press, devoted to education. Inevitably, the resulting pattern is like a patchwork quilt; but it is a price worth paying if it has brought ordinary parents inside the school doors, mentally and often physically, for the first time, instead of leaving them shunned on the outside.

The main alternatives offered in Circular 10/65 were as follows:

1. *Comprehensive schools 11–18.* First in the field, this pattern obviously had to be allowed for in any reorganization. London was committed to it. Already, when the circular was issued, sixty local education authorities in England and Wales were providing one or more secondary schools of this type. In addition to the Isle of Man, three authorities had a completely comprehensive organization of 11–18 schools: Anglesey, Merioneth and Montgomery. The schools in existence ranged in size from around 200 (in rural Wales) to 2,000 (in London), and more than half had fewer than 1,000 pupils.

2. *Comprehensive schools 11–16, followed by comprehensive sixth form college 15/16–18/19.* Entry to such colleges must clearly be open to all, regardless of the possession of GCE, or CSE passes, if they are to be truly comprehensive; though in practice few boys and girls would wish to continue their full-time education without some such indication that they would be likely to profit from it.

Because experience of such an organization was extremely limited at the time, the Circular was cautious about its possibilities. Virtually the only English examples were at Mexborough in the West Riding, where a sixth form college accommodated the grammar school's sixth form and also those boys and girls over fifteen from nearby 'modern' schools who wished to continue their education; the independent international Atlantic College, on the coast of Glamorgan, for boys aged sixteen to nineteen; and the War Office's Welbeck College. Unfortunately the Croydon plan, mooted eleven years before, had failed to get off the ground; but the idea had taken root, and by 1965 several authorities were already planning reorganization on this basis.

3. *Junior and senior comprehensive schools, together covering the 11–18 range, with transfer of all children from one to the other at either 13 or 14.* Such an arrangement is a logical development from the Leicestershire experiment. It is attractive on practical grounds, because existing 'modern' schools can be converted into junior comprehensives fairly easily, and grammar schools into senior comprehensives. On the other hand it is unwelcome to 'modern' schools which have already developed GCE and CSE courses. Two-year schools (11–13) have been described as 'transit camps', while a break at 14 is usually considered to come too near the time when external examinations

have to be taken, after little more than a year and two terms.

4. *Three-tier comprehensive schooling: e.g. 5–9, 9–13, 13–18.* There is an obvious parallel here with the independent school system, since preparatory schools normally take pupils aged 8/9–13/14, 'public' schools pupils aged 13–18. So long as the law required transfer from primary to secondary education between 10½ and 12 the case for such a pattern in the State system was bound to remain theoretical; but such was the interest in it that in 1964 the law had been changed to make possible the creation of middle schools to accommodate the older primary and the younger secondary school pupils.

These (with latitude for variants such as the starting of secondary education at 12 instead of 11) were the basic alternatives offered by Circular 10/65. In addition, however, it was prepared to approve as temporary expedients plans, like Leicestershire's, Doncaster's or Bradford's, which relied on parents' choice for the transfer of pupils from a lower to a higher school: e.g. junior high schools 11–15 or 11–16, initially recruiting all local children, from which transfer to senior high or grammar school (13/14–18) is made at the age of either 13 or 14; or, after two years in an intermediate school (11–13), to either a 13–16 or a 13–18 school. Such plans could not form a permanent part of a comprehensive system, however, for Leicestershire's experience had already made it clear that under optional transfer the children of middle class parents get a better chance than do children of working class parents.

Such were the alternatives which had to be considered by each and every one of the 163 Local Education Authorities in England and Wales, in addition to 44 Excepted Districts and many more Divisional Executives. The local circumstances of all were different and unique in some degree; yet some approach to a common pattern was necessary.

Four years after the issue of the Circular the picture is still confused. The plans of many local authorities have been delayed: some by the magnitude and complexity of their task; some by the sweeping Conservative victories in the local elections of 1967 and 1968 which led to reconsideration, and occasionally withdrawal, of schemes submitted under Labour control; and many by the Government's own financial restrictions. It was ironical that a Labour Government had to say categorically that no money could be provided to aid comprehensive reorganization as such, the reform it had itself initiated. Many councils, eager nevertheless to go ahead, wove the attainment of their comprehensive goals into the arrangements for raising the school leaving age promised for 1970–1. When the axe fell here comprehensive reform was severely set back, though the release of some funds from 1969 onwards, to facilitate preparations for raising the leaving age in 1972–3, has softened the blow a little.

Nevertheless, frustrated by its colossal economic difficulties, the Labour Government has been unable to prosecute effectively a reform which is not only dear to it, but which has also won the support of the country as a whole.

2. THE PRESENT SCENE

THE Department of Education and Science has estimated that in January 1969 there would be about 880 comprehensive schools run by about 93 of the 163 local education authorities, of whom 22 had gone completely comprehensive. The 1970 forecast is 975 schools run by 95 authorities (25 completely reorganized). For 1971 the corresponding figures are 1,180, 105 and 30.

How satisfactory is this rate of progress?

When the Labour Government announced its acceptance

of the comprehensive principle, a percipient group of people realized that this was far from being the end of the story. They formed the Comprehensive Schools Committee, with the object of monitoring developments, pressing the Government to go forward if its courage should flag, and keeping the public informed about what progress was actually being made.

The state of reorganization

Prominent among the members of this committee is Caroline Benn, wife of the present Minister of Technology. In 1968 the Comprehensive Schools Committee published her survey of the latest position regarding reorganization. On the basis of earlier figures and current trends, and of up-to-date information from local education authorities, she estimated that in the school year 1968–9 about twenty-six per cent of all State secondary school pupils would be in schools which were officially designated as comprehensive : 736,000 pupils in 920 schools. Mrs Benn's investigation, brought up to date by a Government statement in the House of Commons (24 October 1968), revealed that seven of the 163 LEAs were open rebels against the Government's policy, having refused even to submit plans for reorganization: Bournemouth, Bury, Kingston-upon-Thames, Richmond-upon-Thames, Rutland, Westmorland, and Worcester. Another twenty-four Authorities were (October 1968) dragging their feet, in that eleven were still without definite plans, seven had had their schemes rejected by the Department of Education and Science as unsatisfactory, and six had withdrawn schemes previously submitted.

Mrs Benn's survey showed that many of the remaining 132 Authorities had plans for only part of their areas, or had plans but no starting dates, or intended selection for local grammar schools to continue alongside comprehensive schemes. She further estimated that twenty-eight per cent of the secondary schools were not yet involved in plans at all. Her conclusions prevent anyone from becoming complacent:

Bearing in mind that many of the Authorities most anxious and willing to reorganize will have done so by 1970, while those that remain will tend to be the more unwilling or unenthusiastic; and bearing in mind that this table does not show up the effects of the cuts and restrictions of January 1968 but only the effects of Circular 10/65, and that the effect of these cuts is likely to show up from 1969/70 on; and bearing in mind that many of these schemes are selective and interim only, is it good enough that only one-quarter of secondary school pupils should be in comprehensive schools almost five years after a government was first elected with a clear mandate for national reorganization, almost four years after that policy was implemented by Circular 10/65, and a full quarter of a century after the introduction of comprehensive schools into Britain by Local Education Authorities? The answer must certainly be that it is not good enough.

And again:

Three years after reorganization plans were requested and two years after plans were definitely asked to be in, well over a quarter of secondary schools are without any plans at all – even for the year 2000. Once again the question, is this good enough? And once again the answer must be that it is not.

These are severe strictures, but they err on the generous side if we take into account the evidence presented on p. 107 below, which indicates that at least a quarter of the schools which are commonly called 'comprehensive' cannot reasonably be accepted as such. This suggests that the number of pupils in really comprehensive schools in 1968–9 was still under twenty per cent.

Mrs Benn also examined the nature of the schemes for reorganization which have so far been prepared. Her study revealed that (1) thirty-eight per cent of the schools are to be of the orthodox 11–18 kind; (2) thirty-two per cent will involve transfer at 16 (i.e. twenty-two per cent in an arrangement of 11–16 schools co-existing with 11–18, plus ten per cent in sixth form colleges); (3) only ten per cent will be Leicestershire-style, with junior/senior comprehensive schools and transfer at 13 or 14; but (4) an impressive twenty per cent are to be based on the middle school idea (9–13, 13–18). Thus plans (2) and (4), starting from nothing and given the most lukewarm recognition in the Circular, have quickly assumed great importance. It is certain that more Authorities will plump for one or the other – and this brings to the fore an issue of great educational significance.

Fundamentally the question is whether transfer should normally be at 13 or at 16. If the former, we assume that secondary education should occupy the years 13–18, as in the independent system and, hitherto, in the State system. If the latter, we are saying that pupils of 16 and over should be regarded as students rather than schoolchildren. Moreover, the new thinking is leading some Authorities to the conclusion that, if schooling is to end at 16, the natural home of all 16–18-year-olds should be the institution which for years has catered successfully for many of those who left school at 15 or 16: the local college of further education or technical college. Such an arrangement has already been approved by two Authorities in the south-west, Exeter and Devon (the latter for Barnstaple and district).

The position and the problem are stated here; their implications for the future will be considered in my final chapter. Meanwhile, the experience of two other countries, Canada and Sweden, is particularly relevant to our own position.

Lessons from Canada

Canada has had separate junior and senior high schools in different provinces since 1927, as well as orthodox comprehensive schools. But in Ontario and British Columbia, where both two-tier and orthodox comprehensive schools are common and well-tried, I found no agreement about their respective merits. I talked with Dr David Gaitskell, himself a former junior-high-school principal, a cousin of the late Hugh Gaitskell. He favoured the two-tier pattern. Others plumped for continuity of schooling throughout adolescence.

In favour of separate junior/senior high schools one hears three main claims:

1. The junior high school helps children to make a gradual transition from the all-purpose class teacher of the primary school to the many specialist teachers of the secondary school. At North York about two thirds of the first year timetable in the junior high school is taught by the form teacher, in the second year one third. In the third year, normal secondary-school specialist teaching obtains.

2. In the junior high school, boys and girls can remain boys and girls, and avoid the sophisticated influence of older pupils. They are happier, too, because they have a bigger say in the running of their own affairs; and the intimacy of the small community is particularly important during adolescence. In the same way, a senior high school is a more mature grown-up community, which older adolescents find more acceptable than an ordinary school.

3. A bigger range of optional courses can be provided in a senior high school than in a 'through' school of the same size.

On the other side the main arguments are these :

1. A break after only three years is harmful. Some pupils take the better part of a year to adjust to their new teachers and the new environment in a senior high school. Continuity and undisturbed growth are essential in the education of adolescents.

2. It is the junior-high-school boys and girls who at fourteen and fifteen are the most flighty and least responsible. They need the steadying influence and example of the seventeen- and eighteen-year-olds.

3. The standard of teaching and the personal quality of teachers in the junior high schools tends to be average and rather mediocre. The influence of the real scholar is needed, both among his colleagues and on the most gifted pupils.

Sweden[1]

The best example for the planners of a flexible system of comprehensive schools is perhaps that of Sweden. In 1950, after years of careful study, a great programme of educational reform was introduced. It is being implemented gradually, and is under continual review.

The essential feature of the Swedish plan is the basic three-year stage. Schooling begins at seven, and the stages are seven to ten, ten to thirteen, and thirteen to sixteen. There is no formal move from primary to secondary education, from one approach to another. The curriculum and the teaching of one stage blend into those of the next.

From the administrator's viewpoint this gradual build-up has great advantages. It means that, making use of existing buildings, schools suited to different age ranges can be linked together in various patterns according to

1. See Marklund and Söderberg, *The Swedish Comprehensive School* (Longmans, 1968).

local circumstances. For example, there may be some schools providing for a double range, such as seven to thirteen or ten to sixteen. Occasionally, in a remote district, one might have one school for ages seven to sixteen. Such administrative flexibility requires agreement among teachers about certain basic work at each stage, e.g. the main ground to be covered in mathematics and science.

The Swedish reform has been made easier than similar reform in England by the fact that the Swedish *gymnasium*, or grammar school, normally covers the fifteen-to-nineteen age group only. For the present, common education runs to fifteen rather than sixteen, and beyond fifteen the paths diverge into academic, technical, and general courses.

A report by Torsten Husén and Nils-Eric Svensson, of the University of Stockholm, should encourage English scholars to make similar comparative studies.[1] In 1954 comprehensive schools were introduced on the south side of Stockholm while two types of secondary school were retained on the north side. Full records were available to indicate the social class from which all the children aged ten-plus came, and the whole of this age group took tests of their intelligence, attainment, and attitudes to future schooling. Since that time. Husén and Svensson have re-tested samples of the original age group.

Their provisional conclusions, now confirmed, 'run counter to the opinion held by many educators, at least in Sweden, that it is the able children who are most handicapped by being taught in undifferentiated classes'. They say that: 1. on the south side of the city, the kind of children who would previously have gone to the *realskola* (academic school) have not suffered from being in a comprehensive school: their progress is similar to that of com-

1. *The School Review* (University of Chicago Press, Spring 1960), pp. 36–51, 'Pedagogic Milieu and Development of Intellectual Skills'.

parable children in *realskola* on the north side; 2. children from poorer homes have responded most strongly to the superior advantages of the comprehensive school over the Swedish equivalent of the 'modern' school : there is nothing to be said for grouping together children of average and below-average capacity. In 1965 Professor Husén was able to say :

It was found that the comprehensive system had a greater total yield by the age of fifteen than the selective one. On the whole bright pupils performed better in the selective system at an early age but by the age of fifteen there was no difference, whereas poorer ability pupils performed better in the comprehensive system.[1]

Urban Dahlof, however, has since shown that much depends on the teaching methods used in Sweden's unstreamed classes.

The rural areas

The provision of comprehensive schools in England, outside London, falls into two distinct categories. First in time, and in recruitment more comprehensive than anything London and the other big cities can show, come the rural areas, especially the rural areas of the north-west.

The evolution of comprehensive education in these places owes little or nothing to educational, social, or political theories. It has been a matter of hard economics and practical efficiency. When 'secondary education for all' was decreed in 1944, most of them had only their little grammar schools, often of 100–200 pupils, to do the job. The other eleven-to-fourteen-year-olds were still in village elementary schools – indeed, the last traces of these 'all-age' schools have still not been swept away. There were no junior-technical or senior-elementary schools to tempt

1. Address to the American Educational Research Association in Chicago.

education committees to take the easy way out; the paper creation of new types of secondary education by writing large the old elementary forms was not possible here.

There was evidence enough in the 1940s that these small grammar schools were too small to do properly, especially at sixth form (i.e. advanced) level, even the limited job of giving an academic education to a select minority. Indeed, grammar schools of 300–500 were also inadequate in important ways. A survey which I made of twenty-one grammar schools in a midland area in 1948 showed that the average sixth form consisted of twenty-five first-year students, fourteen second-year, and four third-year. Classes of one or two pupils were common, and in forty-five per cent of the courses the first-year and second-year classes had to be taught together. Only English and French could be taken to advanced level (in those days the Higher Certificate) at every grammar school; music was not available to this standard in ten schools, biology in five, geography in three.

A national survey[1] brought out the deplorable state of affairs in the fifty-nine smallest grammar schools, each with fewer than 200 pupils:

First, second, and even third-year sixth formers have often to be taken together. 'In a small and remote school like this, sixth form work cannot be organized really efficiently,' concludes more than one head.

The basic equipment of books, laboratories, and specialist teachers – particularly in the sciences – was often sadly lacking. The situation in schools then thought of as medium-sized (200–500) was little better:

'Our sixth-form work is crippled by lack of staff and accommodation. We have only one laboratory for 250 children ... We cannot separate the first and second year sixth, or principal

1. *The Times Educational Supplement*, 15 and 29 July 1949.

and subsidiary classes, and cannot offer the alternatives I would like. Six periods, for example, are given to sixth-form French, and in that class are four separate divisions among seven children.'

Clearly it was absurd to think of building small 'modern' schools parallel to the existing little grammar schools, and so multiplying inefficiency. A more sensible course was to bring all children of secondary age under one roof. More teachers, more variously qualified, could thus be available to help to educate all the children. At the same time it was possible, at less overall expense, to build better schools, provide more and better equipment, and offer a greater range of courses to meet the different needs of a complete age-group.

The education authority of the Isle of Man (which is not a county, and has its own government and educational system), and such counties as the North and East Ridings, Anglesey, Merioneth, Cardigan, Montgomery, Brecon, Dorset and Devon made possible a commonsense rural organization which is now accepted without question by everyone.

This rural reorganization has, wherever possible, taken the form simply of enlarging in every way – numbers, range of courses, educational opportunity – an established grammar school. It may have to be re-housed in new buildings, but the school lives on, and indeed has invariably found fresh vigour. Its roots are more firm, reaching to and drawing from the whole local community. It can readily become the cultural heart of the market town and district, in a two-way flow of ideas and activities, knitting local society together.

Here is a prospect of completing the vision of Henry Morris, formerly chief education officer for Cambridgeshire, embodied in the village colleges of that county. Between the wars Morris added adult wings and adult tutors to his senior elementary schools; he used buses to bring people in to these centres from surrounding villages and hamlets in the evenings and at weekends, and he encouraged the outflow of tutors and other help to those villages. But there was one big gap in his plan: some of the best brains were withdrawn at eleven and sent to the city for a specialized grammar-school education. The American philosopher, Baker Brownell, warned his countrymen against thus bleeding the talent of small communities.[1] In the rural comprehensive school, that does not happen.

I write of 'prospect' rather than 'achievement' as yet, though real progress is now being made. Thus at Castletown, in the Isle of Man, Castle Rushen High School acts at once as a focal point for the cultural life of the area – all the southern part of the Island – and as a fertilizing agent in the little town and surrounding villages. For example, parents and friends join in the school orchestra; children in turn are members of local bands and music societies. This interaction goes on in a number of ways. Not least important is the constant informal consultation between teachers and parents about individual children.

Only in a relatively small community, one in which all the children are known not only as individuals but as members of a family who are themselves well known, is this possible. The teachers in turn are known by children and parents not only as teachers but as men and women who may join them in the cricket or football team, at whist drives, or on any other local occasion. Mutual confidence is established; and a richer, deeper education than can ever be bred in the classroom alone is the result.

But we still have too few Castle Rushens. All too often the school closes down when the buses leave at four o'clock. Some cricket and football fields remain empty all the week-end and holidays, while young men and boys

1. *The Human Community* (Harper, New York, 1951).

struggle to play well in rough pastures. There are not enough home-and-school associations. Contact between teachers, parents, and other people of the district may be rare and haphazard. There is much still to be done.

I believe that rural society, apathetic though it may seem – as living things commonly are when suffering from malnutrition – needs and thirsts for new life. A bigger, more dynamic conception of the role of the rural comprehensive school would help to make it possible. The natives of Roman Britain were in the habit of dedicating their altars to 'the genius of the place'. That genius is still a powerful force, readily commanding group loyalties and communal effort.

It is significant that the enlargement of rural grammar schools into comprehensive schools, while retaining their old name, has been widely welcomed by local people. Abolition of the eleven-plus bogy is, of course, an obvious relief. But beyond that, we must realize that country society is today far less stratified than town society; if there is to be secondary education for all, enforced segregation in different types of school is an artificial instrument which makes little sense to the villager.

The life of any individual is short, but the life of such established communities is long: communal roots are deep, communal memories drift persistently through the centuries. It is well to remember that the rural comprehensive school merely puts right a modern aberration. Basically it is a reversion to the conditions of the seventeenth century, when many grammar schools were 'free' schools, and open to all the children of the district. For example at Moulton Grammar School, in Lincolnshire, the schoolmaster was not compelled to admit or teach any scholar who could not already read:

Nevertheless it is to be wished that he will not refuse any of the town of Moulton that will come to the school, but suffer them to learn what they can amongst the rest of the scholars, or by the help of some other.[1]

For Windermere Grammar School, lately a very small comprehensive school for boys, the wheel has come full circle. The first deeds (1613) said that the school was to be free to local inhabitants, but not to outsiders; and the scholars were to be instructed in 'gramar, writing and reading and other good learninge and discipline meete and convenient for them . . .'[2] No minimum standard of attainment appears to have been required before a pupil was admitted. Today, the tiny schools of Windermere and Kelsick have been merged in a Lakes comprehensive school of 600 boys and girls which, while meeting modern needs, will strengthen the bonds between school and community and carry on the old traditions.

Fundamentally, then, the rural comprehensive school is sound. But it has one main weakness: its inability to provide at sixth-form level, economically and efficiently, a range of courses wide enough to meet the very different needs of all its pupils. For the country school is necessarily quite small. Figures obtained during 1968–9 from a sample of them show that on average some twenty-six per cent of each age-group stayed at school for a sixth year, sixteen per cent for a seventh year. This means, in a rural school of 650, about thirty-one pupils in the first year of the sixth form, nineteen in the second year.[3]

Such small numbers would not matter – they might even be an advantage – if general education up to eighteen were

1. *Orders and Regulations governing Moulton Grammar School*, 1599.

2. *Windermere Grammar School: A History* (Westmorland Gazette, Kendal, 1936).

3. Monks' N.F.E.R. survey (*Comprehensive Education in England and Wales*, 1968) found that in 1966 the average size of a sixth form in schools of 600 or fewer pupils was 40.

accepted policy in England; but it is not. Sixth-form students must specialize in two, three, or four subjects if they wish to go to college or university. The liberal educationist, who wants schools to meet the greatly varying needs of individual pupils, favours neither the restriction of all to a common curriculum nor enforced early specialization. What he must recognize is the advantage of a school's being able to provide, especially for older pupils, a considerable range of optional subjects: technical, commercial, practical, academic, and cultural.

In practice, the situation is this: that the rural comprehensive school offers a reasonably adequate range of courses up to GCE ordinary level (taken at fifteen or sixteen) or to the Certificate of Secondary Education. Such a curriculum normally includes the following subjects, with an opportunity to drop any given subject from fourteen to sixteen and emphasize others, but no real specialization: English, French, Latin, history, geography, mathematics, biology, chemistry, physics, art, music, housecraft (girls), and woodwork and metalwork (boys). Occasionally a school will introduce commercial subjects at the 14-16 stage, but this practice is less common in the country than in the towns. Optional courses in agriculture or horticulture may also be available.

At the sixth-form stage, however, it is usually a different story. Some small schools do offer a pretty full programme of up to eighteen subjects, but ten to fifteen subjects is much more common. Yet country boys and girls must not be denied opportunity comparable to that of town children. The potential gap is most readily explained by listing the kind of sixth-form curriculum from which a pupil attending a large, new, well-provided urban comprehensive school may choose:

English; modern languages (French, German, Russian, Spanish); classics (Latin, Greek, ancient history); geography; history;

economics; pure and applied mathematics; sciences (botany, zoology, chemistry, physics); art and architecture; domestic subjects (needlework, cookery, hygiene, etc.); pre-nursing courses; commercial subjects (accountancy, shorthand, typing, commercial geography and economics); engineering; technical drawing; heavy crafts (building, woodwork, metalwork); music.

I would agree that say twelve subjects judiciously chosen from the above list (e.g. English, French, German, Latin, history, geography, biology, chemistry, physics, mathematics, art, music) afford a not unreasonable choice for most members of the kind of sixth form we know in the grammar schools; but today that is not enough. Although we still have our academic pupils, they are being joined by others whose eyes are not set on universities, whose interests and needs range wider but are no less important than those of the intellectual pupil.

Even when a small school does, most nobly, extend its sixth-form curriculum to meet this challenge, it is inevitable that many classes will consist of only one or two pupils, and that some pupils at different stages of their work will have to be taught together. Classes can be too small for educational efficiency, as well as too big. At this stage the optimum size is perhaps eight to twelve : small enough for each pupil to get individual attention from the teacher, and big enough to encourage the cross-fertilization of ideas within the group – one of the most potent factors in learning.

Can we afford the extravagant use of scarce highly-qualified staff – an extravagance not matched nowadays even by the universities – which the small sixth form entails? Can the expensive items of equipment now essential for advanced studies in science and technology be used sufficiently, in this situation, to justify their provision? Will not a local education authority be very naturally inclined to economize here – and by so doing restrict the education which ought to be available to all its young people? It may, of course, be argued that it is the duty of the local authority to prime the pump, and that if extra staff, equipment and courses were provided, more and more pupils would stay to take advantage of them.

That, indeed, is happening to some extent. Nevertheless the question posed earlier, as to whether education beyond sixteen ought to be given in school or in some separate institution, is highlighted by the problems of the rural secondary school.

The towns: new centres of population

Outside the rural areas, the impulse towards comprehensive schooling has been very different in origin and has followed a much more stormy course. The enlargement of the country grammar school was seen to be the logical, sensible way of providing for rural communities which were little concerned about the refinements of social status. The problem in the towns, where large, efficient, selective schools (grammar and sometimes technical too) were entrenched, was much greater.

The grammar schools' great prestige gave them a powerful and pervasive voice in national affairs. Their old scholars, inevitably, often held responsible positions in local government, the local Press, industry, and commerce. Old boys and old girls, former teachers and headmasters, were all filled with a nostalgic affection for *alma mater* who had helped to make them what they were. As parents in a status-conscious society, they were naturally anxious that their children in turn should have at least the 'advantages' which they had themselves enjoyed; and they were joined in this desire by those worthy working-class parents who hoped to see *their* children move out of the pit or the factory and get a white-collar job. Almost all these people favoured selection for grammar schools – provided their children were among the selected.

Here, however, was the first chink in the defences of the existing order. As the years went by, the number of disappointed and vocal parents inevitably grew. On the sidelines stood many influential products of the independent schools, which had never paid much regard to selection by ability anyway. Quite a lot of them were sympathetic to the comprehensive idea. At first they watched as though it were a street fight which did not really concern them; but the bolder spirits have one by one declared themselves on the side of the reformers. The cutting edge of the attack on eleven plus and the segregated system, however, came from those sociologists and psychologists who dissected its weaknesses and held up its fallibility for all to see. They established a position of strength from which reform could come.

Repeatedly, however, England has preferred evolution to revolution. Our rulers' most masterly tactics, over the centuries, have been the ordered retreat, the skilful, gradual, unnoticed shifting of position, the absorption of the ideas of the reformers, and ultimately – suitably modified and maybe under a new guise – their adoption.

This is what has happened in English secondary education. In view of mounting popular pressure and the growing weight of expert evidence, it would have been suicidal for any Government to ban comprehensive schools altogether. Indeed, I am sure that the process of strategic withdrawal, of cushioning and absorbing the attack, is often an unconscious one. It is revealing to look back a mere eight years to an obviously sincere statement by a former H.M. Senior Chief Inspector of Schools, Percy Wilson:

This [the organization of secondary education] is a matter where most of us have been emotionally involved and I think we are most of us guilty, in the past, of having said some foolishly dogmatic things. I know I have. We have taken sides on *a priori* grounds, in ignorance or partial ignorance of the real criteria of judgement. . . . There is room for co-existence. I would go further – there is *need* for co-existence.[1]

So, under Conservative rule, we had the policy of Sir David Eccles, laid down during his first period of office. This was: to accept the case for rural comprehensive schools and to allow new comprehensives to be provided, where the local education authority wished it, in new centres of population such as the new towns and housing estates; but to draw the line at changing the character of established grammar schools in towns and cities by enlarging or absorbing them into comprehensive schools.

Conservative policy entailed a further handicap for comprehensive schools. It is well known that the cultural background of most of the people who move from city slums to new council housing estates is distinctly poorer than that of a cross-section of the nation. When the Minister insisted, as he did, that children within a comprehensive school's catchment area had the right to try for a grammar school place, and to accept it if they were successful, the loss of these few was a grievous blow to the local school. It might fill their places with children of nearly comparable ability from outside the normal catchment area who had just missed a grammar school place, or whose parents preferred them to attend a comprehensive school. But this did not compensate for the effect on the school's local prestige when the brightest children went elsewhere.

Almost all the urban comprehensives suffer to some extent in this way from creaming by the grammar schools or from the one-class background of nearly all the children

1. *Views and Prospects from Curzon Street*, 1961, pp. 16–17.

on those housing estates which result from slum clearance. The best example of the latter situation is the Z-Cars estate of Kirkby, near Liverpool.

Fundamentally Kirkby's problem is lack of roots and social stability. Within ten years the 1952 village of 1,200 people, with 134 schoolchildren and five teachers, was transformed into a town of 52,000 with 16,600 schoolchildren and 648 teachers. At first the schools were constantly in flux as new children drifted in. The growth of the new town is now, however, largely complete, with a population more or less stabilized at 65,000. Nearly all the families were shifted from the crowded inner wards of Liverpool. More than half were Roman Catholic, but large families of four, five, six or more were the rule, irrespective of religious affiliation. As in so many estates the emphasis was on housing almost regardless of the need for community buildings, and the result was a tale of destruction from anti-social behaviour.

The health of many families on the estate is below average, and school attendance is difficult to enforce. The juvenile court is all too familiar to many children. The need not only for a community centre, but for leadership from such a centre, is very great – and it must serve families as well as individuals, adults and teen-age workers as well as children.

There are four comprehensive schools, each for about 2,000 pupils: two county mixed schools (Brookfield and Ruffwood) and two Roman Catholic (St Gregory's for girls and St Kevin's for boys). All are responding to the challenge in two main ways: first, by creating self-respect in pupils (and their parents) for their own educational abilities, and with it respect for the school; secondly, by giving that positive social leadership which the community desperately needs.

Professor Mays and his colleagues have turned the spot-

light on one of these four schools, Ruffwood.[1] They depict
a firm but kindly and imaginative head, supported by a
staff on the whole younger and more socially committed
than most. The average ability of the children, as
measured by the accepted tests, is low : the average intelligence quotient of the 1959 entry was only 86 (national
average 100), English quotient 82, arithmetic quotient 87.
Only eight children who entered the school in that year
could be rated as being of grammar school ability. But of
this same intake eleven were to gain passes at GCE Advanced level in three or four subjects, six in two subjects,
and eight in one subject; and, from the same year, ten
pupils went forward to read for a university degree, twelve
to colleges of education. Later results have been similarly
impressive.

Mays describes an extensive programme of out-of-
school activities organized by the teachers of Ruffwood
School. He notes, too, that against expectations close on a
dozen teachers are now living in the area – a development
which, if the trend continues, must strengthen the contribution which the school can make to the life of the
community. On the other hand he pinpoints what may be
the most serious handicap for schools in districts such as
this: that (in terms of the Registrar-General's socio-economic
scale) a predominantly middle-class group of teachers is
trying to educate predominantly working-class children.
There are alien standards and values separating the two.
It says much for Ruffwood that (in Mays' judgement) as
many as

a third of the teachers, especially those in senior positions, were
actively aware of both the moral and the social difficulties
implicit in their role.... They were also much more committed to thoroughgoing change and social reform than the

1. Mays, Quine and Pickett, *School of Tomorrow* (Longmans, 1968).

majority who tended to be critical of the community and who wished only to raise its standards.

This gulf between the middle class and the working class is not one which can be bridged merely by throwing the two together in the difficult circumstances of any school in any area like Kirkby. There is urgent need of a radical overhaul of the whole philosophy and process of the education of teachers in colleges and universities. And we must start from such a premise as that given by Professor Mays: the need to find for working class children

a kind of school that makes sense to them, a school which does not ask them to break faith with their own loyalties and traditions and which, at the same time, is in no sense academically second rate. This is, in fact, what Ruffwood has been trying to do, with results which so far are encouraging, and the next years of its history should see the process brought even closer to fulfilment.

When we turn from Kirkby to the new town of Crawley in Sussex we enter a different world. It is in such counties that the professional classes swarm, and their first demand is for high academic standards. The Thomas Bennett School has provided them: from the first intake three pupils won scholarships to Oxford or Cambridge, and thirty-one per cent (against a national average of thirteen per cent) gained five or more passes at GCE Ordinary level. By 1968–9 seven children out of ten were choosing to stay at school for a fifth year, more than one in three for a sixth year.

With that comforting reputation firmly established, the school is now able to initiate pioneer work in the curriculum and in social organization, such as experiments in non-streaming, which might earlier have disturbed the more conventional customers. Basically the aims of Thomas Bennett and Ruffwood are the same: scholarship of high quality, and the creation of an environment rich in opportunity, inviting the happy participation of every child.

These aims need, however, to be much more clearly understood by teachers and parents, by officers and members of education committees. Only so can we make the rapid, efficient progress in the building of an effective schools system which the welfare of the nation requires as a top priority.

Coventry is less fortunate. One of the pioneers in setting up a network of schools which were intended to be comprehensive, and were indeed so called, it has still not succeeded in removing the major obstacle to their full development. Two direct grant boys' grammar schools and two maintained girls' grammar schools together take perhaps ninety per cent of the most able children in the city. At the other end of the scale, nine secondary 'modern' schools remain to prop up the league table. In a forceful article printed in *Forum* (May 1969) Mr H. H. Tilley, head of Caludon Castle School, exposes this graded system which makes the so-called comprehensives a permanent second-best and preserves indefinitely the evils of the eleven-plus for the children and parents of Coventry. Today, he claims, 'the doors and windows are more tightly shut than at any time during the last fifteen years,' and he demands that honesty at least requires that such schools as his should cease to be called 'comprehensive'. The same demand was voiced in an earlier edition of *Forum*, in relation to London's so-called 'comprehensive' schools, by the late E. E. McCarthy.

One major problem of urban reorganization remains to be considered. Circular 10/65 urged authorities 'to ensure, when determining catchment areas, that schools are as socially and intellectually comprehensive as is practicable': i.e. they should strive to get some balance in the socio-economic background of the pupils. On the other hand the different social classes tend, by and large, to live in different districts.

This is a world-wide problem. For example at Haifa, on Mount Carmel in Israel, the poor live down by the docks, the lower-middle classes half way up the slope, and the rich on top. In America the problem is made still more acute because the poor are usually to be equated with the coloured; and England already faces this embarrassment in several cities.

An artificial mix of social classes, with a fair spread of measured intelligence, can be obtained by transferring all the children who are leaving primary schools X, Y and Z, situated in districts which are all different in social character, to one secondary school. It will often mean, however, longer bus journeys for the children and an increase in already crowded city traffic for the public. Moreover it is open to some objection as an attempt to impose middle-class values on transplanted groups of working-class children, who might often feel out of place and respond below their true capacity.

Such a device would mean the destruction of the idea of the comprehensive school as a social and cultural centre for all local people. Vital to this concept is ease of contact between home and school, and close collaboration between parents and teachers who know each other – not only over their children's welfare, but in their own lives as members of a vigorous common community. Because they have never been so identified, but have drawn their pupils from a minority of homes over a wide geographical field, grammar schools have usually been self-sufficient communities; and the comprehensive schools of London are open to similar criticism. It would be a sad limitation of the comprehensive idea, and indeed of the character which many schools have already developed, if this concept of the neighbourhood school were to be sacrificed.

The right answer must be to stick to the comprehensive school as the school for all children of the district, but where such a district clearly falls short of the cultural advantages enjoyed by better-off people to compensate (so far as a school can) by providing better buildings and facilities, more and better teachers. Plowden has recommended the same idea for primary schools. Incentives can be worked out without too much difficulty; and if good work in such neighbourhoods is recognized both financially and as likely to lead to promotion, some of the finest teachers in the country, particularly among the young, will be attracted.

At the same time we must acknowledge that compensatory education by itself will never be enough. The Coleman Report in the U.S.A. suggests that the quality of the other children in the school may be more important even than the standard of teaching, certainly more important than buildings, curriculum and size of class. So, if we are to have good neighbourhood schools, we must create socially integrated neighbourhoods, using all the agencies of government (especially planning and housing) at our disposal. The problem cannot be solved by the educators alone.

London

It was Hitler and Göring, with all their evil apparatus of war, who made possible London's educational 'new look'. Not only did they damage or destroy 1,150 out of the 1,200 schools and departments, but they provoked in the people of the capital a reforming zeal, a vision of a better world, which in this century has been one of the curious compensations thrown up by savage destruction. Decades of slothful peace do not, alas, achieve so much.

The practical expression of this idealism came in the County of London Plan – a great sociological document which foreshadowed a proud and busy future for each of London's neighbourhoods and boroughs, knit harmoniously in a cooperative whole. The London School Plan, adopted by the County Council in March 1947 and approved by the Minister of Education in February 1950, was a necessary complement to the larger scheme. In particular, the decision to rebuild secondary education on the basis of comprehensive schools was a powerful reinforcement to the idea of neighbourhood communities.

During 1946–9 eight experimental comprehensive schools were established. Their buildings were old and sometimes separated by more than one street, for new secondary-school building was not then permitted. All the pupils had fallen at the great eleven-plus hurdle, education's Becher's Brook. Working in depressing material conditions, both teachers and pupils needed limitless faith and encouragement. Parents, too, had to be convinced that the new aims were worth while; and this was made no easier by the stream of lordly condemnation which poured from eminent but ill-informed lips and was given prominence in the national press.

It was in these circumstances that the calibre of the eight chosen head teachers was tested and vindicated. They were the pioneers who hewed a path through the jungle of obscurantism and cultural poverty. I recall most vividly – no other word is appropriate – Miss O'Reilly of Walworth. The Irish are at their best when fighting against odds, whether in Connemara or the Congo. Here was one of the first women heads of mixed schools, the flame of whose idealism, energy, and love fired many of those children, and their teachers and parents, with faith in themselves and in their school. There were others too, who in their different ways paved the way for the handsome, assured Kidbrookes and Tulse Hills of the future.

It was at these 'interim comprehensives' that individual children began, most startlingly, to shatter general belief in the validity of eleven-plus selection and the relative permanence of the 'intelligence quotient' (I.Q.). 'Jean Smith', for example, started in the lowest stream of the lowest class with an I.Q. of 96, languished for three years, and then came to life; she passed in seven subjects at GCE ordinary level, including Latin in one year, and went on to become a teacher. 'David Jones', another teacher, came in his fourth year from a local 'modern' school with an I.Q. of 80; two years later he passed in five subjects at GCE ordinary level and went on to study English, history, scripture and music.

Such examples of late development are now almost commonplace. They have always occurred in independent schools, but little notice has been given to examples from this field.[1] It was the earliest comprehensive schools, in London and elsewhere, which furnished much of the ammunition which has shot to shreds the intellectual case for a stratified pattern of education, taken for granted less than twenty years ago.

When London took up the post-war threads, there were four main types of secondary school ripe for reorganization apart from the independent and voluntary grammar schools. They were county grammar schools, 'central' schools for borderline eleven-plus cases, junior technical schools still mostly housed in technical college buildings, and the former senior elementary schools, which took the unfortunate children who had failed to qualify for any of the above types of school. This pattern was gradually changed. Some technical schools have been merged, with much better facilities, in new comprehensive schools. All

1. cf., however, O. M. Slaney, *I.Q. and O Level* (*The Times Educational Supplement* 25 September 1959), who showed that 93% of boys at Lancing College with I.Q.s under 115 gained 'good' GCEs; and L. Bruce Lockhart, letter in *T.E.S.*, 22 September 1961: 'One of the Gresham's pupils who failed at 11+ and 12+, after a full range of O levels got distinction in two A levels plus an alpha in the general paper – a case which is, I am sure, typical of most good public schools.'

the larger secondary schools, whether in old or new buildings, now provide courses of some kind beyond the fourth year.

Other problems were raised by the needs of the churches. Both the Church of England and the Roman Catholics wanted smaller secondary schools than those contemplated by the county, and both wanted some separate grammar schools. Time has modified the opinion of both churches on the question of size, at least, and their schools will in fact be nearer to the Inner London Education Authority (ILEA) norm than was originally planned.

London's main headache, however, has been the voluntary grammar schools, over fifty of them, which could not be disturbed. These schools, whose good academic records and high social prestige naturally attract parents, have continued to tap the full flow of talent which would otherwise have gone to the local comprehensive school. As in Coventry and Bristol, this is a most serious issue. The faith of all but the most ardent socialists has been severely tested when the choice has been local comprehensive school or grammar/'public' school for their own children.

In the neighbourhoods served by voluntary grammar schools, the best the London County Council could do was to provide other secondary schools, each complementary to a voluntary school in educational provision. Naturally these 'county complements' tend to be much smaller (perhaps 750–800) than the schools intended to be fully comprehensive. The latter were commonly planned to take 2,000–2,200 but their numbers are being cut to 1,500–1,900 as London's population moves out beyond its boundaries. The county-complement system is a makeshift business, which in effect accepts the division of secondary education in these districts into 'grammar' and 'sub-comprehensive'.

The innumerable obstacles which have hindered the development of the County of London Plan have also made it extremely difficult for London to pursue effectively the aim of serving each neighbourhood with a comprehensive school. It is perhaps inevitable, but none the less disappointing, to find that London's only definition of 'fully comprehensive' is 'the intention to provide fully and equally for the needs of pupils of all levels of ability'.[1] It means that these schools do not necessarily have a true cross-section of an age-group. More important, it means that a school's catchment area is not a clearly-defined neighbourhood unit. Eltham Green, for example, is a school set up half-way between two townships, but belonging to neither.

In such circumstances a school is forced into a more self-sufficient existence than perhaps the staff themselves would desire. Vigorous school societies abound, and so do parent-teacher associations, but apart from certain schools like Haverstock, Collingwood, Walworth, and Peckham, which stress social service, activity is school-centred; the two-way flow, often involving people other than parents, which marks the real neighbourhood community, is missing. So the school becomes a cultural oasis in the suburban desert. Given the desert, it is invaluable, but in terms of rounded social life it lacks something when compared with a place where school and community are balanced and integrated, such as Castletown or Douglas in the Isle of Man, Thirsk in the North Riding, or the new town of Crawley in Sussex. I recall the London teacher who, concerned at the continued absence of a child from her class, asked the girl's school-friends to call on her and see whether she was ill. But they could not; they did not know where she lived.

A further regrettable consequence of this very limited definition of 'comprehensive' is that more than half of

1. *London Comprehensive Schools* (1961 report), p. 13.

London's new-type schools are for either boys or girls only. In the second half of the twentieth century – when even those conservative bodies the universities are trying out mixed halls of residence – the establishment of new schools on this one-sex basis is deplorable. They can at best be only semi-comprehensive. The real point of the argument for having a school which is a mixed, balanced, healthy, natural community is lost. Such lopsided experience, in an almost exclusively male or female world of up to 2,000 children and adults, cannot be reconciled with the case for an education which is socially complete as well as scholastically sound. On this issue I prefer the definition of comprehensive schools, given by the Department of Education and Science, as 'schools intended for all secondary pupils in a district'.

Throughout the period 1944–62 the eleven-plus examination continued, and on it was based the allocation of pupils to grammar and technical schools, as well as to the different streams of comprehensive schools. Now London has the Junior Leaving examination. Selection has not yet ceased, but in future we may have, as in Anglesey, internal assessment of new pupils in comprehensive schools, and perhaps a special grammar-school entrance examination run by the voluntary grammar schools.

No observer of London's educational scene can fail to be impressed by the size and complexity of the task which faced the country's education committee in 1944 and afterwards, by the zeal with which it has been tackled, and by the degree of success already achieved. Whatever detailed criticisms are made, London's achievement is still a magnificent one.

It is all the more discouraging, then, that the first action by the Conservatives when in 1968 they gained control of the Inner London Education Authority (which replaced the LCC in 1965) was to revise the London plan for a more completely comprehensive system and to announce their intention to preserve most of the existing grammar schools. They further decreed that the children of grammar school ability surplus to the places available in grammar schools should be spread evenly among all the comprehensive schools.

While this helped the least popular comprehensives a little, it spoiled the normal spread of ability which a few of the best known comprehensives, such as Wandsworth and Forest Hill, had painstakingly achieved. It will in future be more difficult for any of the latter to rival the grammar schools, in the academic sphere in particular. There can be little doubt that this act of defiance, from what used to be the heart of the Labour movement, was a main factor in spurring a reluctant Government to consider taking compulsory powers to enforce reorganization on genuinely comprehensive lines.

3. Inside The Schools

I. SIZE, PLACE, WORK

THE doubts concerning comprehensive schools held by the theorists and the men of gold turn on the relative merits of separate types of education on the one hand, common education for all children on the other. Thus the Ministry of Education's first pamphlet, published in 1945, said:

Past experience suggests that schools with a limited and well-defined aim are the most likely to succeed in reaching and maintaining the highest standards within the particular field they serve.

The doubts of the general public are quite different; they practically all turn on fear of one word and its implications: size.

The problem of size

Most adult English people grew up in much smaller societies – towns, villages, schools – than are common today. A recently retired H.M. Senior Chief Inspector of Schools attended a grammar school of 100, which had only three boys in the sixth form. My own grammar school numbered sixty boys when I first went there some forty years ago. Those of us who are migrants from north to midlands or south cherish a nostalgia for the village in the dales, the sturdy cotton or woollen town with a character of its own and a well-defined compass of geographical and social life. The natives of Warwickshire, Sussex, and so on, while prospering from the boom in work and people and property values, at times feel overwhelmed by the incomers. Many of them wistfully recall the independence of the small trader or craftsman which prevailed in their childhood.

Today's picture is very different. Most grammar schools have from 400 to 800 pupils, most 'modern' schools from 300 to 600. It has, however, been a steady growth, to which people have become accustomed gradually.

Twenty years ago, when comprehensive schools first became a public issue, most grammar schools had only 300–500 pupils, most 'modern' schools 100–400. Suddenly the country was confronted with the prospect of new giants which (it was thought) must have at least one thousand pupils to be efficient. A thousand pupils! The figure was the educational equivalent of the sound barrier. (That the barrier was being broken by such respected institutions as Eton College and Manchester Grammar School made little general impact. Such glorious palaces are beyond the ken of common mortals: to us they have the stuff of fairyland or heaven, and therefore we cannot seriously accept them as having any relevance to our daily lives.) Outrage piled on outrage when it appeared that 2,000 rather than 1,000 would be the normal target, if the new schools were to discharge their new role with maximum efficiency. But it's an ill wind that blows no good. Public alarm has made the planners ensure that small social units evolve inside the new communities.

Few would claim complete success for these plans. What new models of houses, cars, refrigerators, find the best answer all at once? And how much more difficult it is to plan for those variable creatures, ourselves! As a Yorkshireman says, 'there's nowt so queer as folk'. Nevertheless, children in comprehensive schools appear to be far more at home, their parents far better pleased and satisfied, than the critics ever expected. Let us look at the present picture.

In the first place, Monks' 1965–6 survey[1] showed that the bogy of big schools is not quite so fearsome in reality

1. *op cit.*, p. 88; information abstracted from Table 4.

as it was in anticipation. Only two out of 331 schools had more than 2,000 pupils. It is true that the size of a good many of today's comprehensive schools, as of other types of school, is scheduled to rise considerably year by year. However, 182 of the 11–18 schools surveyed by Monks were fully developed, and these were distributed as follows:

No. of Schools	No. of Pupils	No. of Schools	No. of Pupils
4	201–400	14	1201–1400
35	401–600	11	1401–1600
24	601–800	11	1601–1800
43	801–1000	10	1801–2000
28	1001–1200	2	More than 2000

The average size of these schools was just under 1,000. The figures show that over a large number of established comprehensive schools the rolls vary evenly from 400 to 2,000. If it can be shown that all such schools are satisfactory, Goliath is slain; there is no longer the need *on educational grounds* for a comprehensive secondary school to be bigger than say 900, though other factors such as shortage of sites may render a larger school necessary or even desirable.

Alas, no such clear-cut generalization seems to me possible. In particularly favourable circumstances, for example with a low pupil/staff ratio and keen parents, a comprehensive school of 500 may be very successful. In other conditions, for example a housing estate where few children stay at school beyond fifteen, where the parents are apathetic and teachers difficult to obtain, a school of 2,000 may find it all it can do to provide adequate sixth-form education.

Such developments as non-streaming, team teaching, language laboratories, programmed learning and correspondence courses make really small comprehensive schools a more viable proposition than they used to appear. Correspondence courses (provided in this country, for example, by the National Extension College) are proving an efficient way of enabling a small school to provide to GCE 'O' or 'A' level such subjects as a second language or economics which may be required only by a very few pupils, or an individual.

We already have a few small comprehensive schools of 200–300: for example a two-form entry school on the roof of the Pennines at Alston, more than one in rural Wales, and the delight of the south-west, the Isles of Scilly school on St Mary's. At present this has 78 children and ten teachers, but it is scheduled to grow to a maximum of 150 children aged 11–16 and 14 teachers. It is also a genuine centre for the community life of the islands.

Recent American research[1] points to social and educational advantages in the small school, and the case for them in England has been well presented by Elizabeth Halsall.[2] Such evidence will be welcomed by all who wish to preserve the vigour and identity of our small country towns. It can no longer be taken for granted that comprehensive reorganization must result in their secondary schools being closed and their children compelled to travel long distances to larger centres of population – particularly if rural comprehensive schools for pupils aged 11–16 are linked with post-16 provision in area colleges.

1. Barker and Gump, *Big School, Small School: High School Size and Student Behaviour* (Stanford Uiversity Press, California, 1964).
2. 'The Small Comprehensive: flexible and open-ended?' in *Comprehensive Education* (Bulletin of the Comprehensive Schools Committee), no. 8, Spring 1968.

The physical environment

In big schools the concourse of some 2,000 children and adults has meant a big challenge to the physical planners of sites and buildings. The physical home of a school is always important, though never so important as the people who inhabit it. On the outskirts of cities some lovely sites have been found, trees have been preserved and planted, architects have often designed gracious buildings. The big headache has been how to reconcile two apparently conflicting needs. On the one hand, space for efficient work, movement, and leisure is needed, room for the individual to breathe and feel uncrowded. On the other, the desire for a school to feel that it is one community calls for buildings compact enough to make communication swift and easy, enabling the head to feel that he is in effective charge, above all ensuring that the children do not feel detached and lost.

In fact, when one thinks of how the buildings – and not only the boarding houses – of great schools like Rugby and Uppingham are scattered over the town, there is by and large little cause for complaint about the layout of comprehensive schools. Of course the architects have sometimes been foolish. A building 180 yards long is as alarming to contemplate as it is tiring to traverse; the lack of covered ways between detached buildings can mean frequent drenching for children and books in wet Wales; cloakrooms may be insufficient at the various points of the school. But most of the obvious defects are the fault not of the architects or the local authority, but of the Government – that is, in the last resort, of ourselves. They are caused by skimping on money, by fearfully costly economy cuts.

In particular, the Department's restriction of circulation space by narrowing corridors and stairs or eliminating them altogether, is most unpopular. These schools are busy places. Everyone there has a job to do, and everyone must move about at certain times to the well-equipped rooms where the job can be done best. This is half the point of having such a school at all. No time-and-motion expert would approve the obstacles, the frustration, even the dangers created by squeezing the traffic so that thousands of minutes in all are wasted every day, hundreds of tempers frayed in one such building.

Great stress is laid by educationists on the social aspect and purpose of comprehensive schools. Here again, a mean money policy inhibits gracious living. How can you rehearse a play to your satisfaction in the assembly-cum-dining hall, while tables are being erected and cutlery laid? How can you pipe a sweet note in the music lesson, when the good ladies on the other side of the hatch, bless them, are humming their juke-box selections?

School dinners were one of the great post-war advances before the teachers most deplorably withdrew from their obligation (it should have been thought of as a right) to participate. They were meant to be more than crude canteen eating. They ought to be civilized occasions when teachers and pupils can talk together over food well cooked (as indeed it is) and nicely served (as it often is not), in rooms and with furniture and tableware which lend dignity and atmosphere to the meal.

Other defects are noted. Not uncommon is complaint about the use of too much glass in new schools with a south or south-west aspect, which causes glare and heat from the sun. Too many schools lack soundproofing. All who control spending on school buildings should have the maddening experience of trying to learn or teach in a room loudly invaded by external noises.

Yet, when all fault-finding is done, one's conclusion must be that these are physically fine schools, pretty well-equipped on the whole for the large new job to be tackled in them. And if the quality of materials and workmanship is not always all it might be, we must beware of going to the other extreme and building marble halls which will last for ever. How many secondary-school buildings put up in say 1933–9 were sufficient for the needs of 1963–9? I know of none which is wholly satisfactory, many which are wholly unsatisfactory.

In all seriousness I suggest that our education officers could do much worse than consult Sir Billy Butlin for advice on how to provide, with speed and economy, functional buildings intended to last for no more than twenty years. A healthy economy would thrive on such a policy, and so would our educational ideas. New ideas should command the means, not wait on them. Coventry, with some aluminium-clad buildings, is an authority which has given a lead in this matter. So, too, has the Department of Education and Science's own team of architects.

The layout, shape, and size of a school's buildings are particularly important, because they often determine the main framework of a school's internal organization. Such decisions on a new school are almost always made by administrator and architect in consultation; teachers are brought in later to work an already-decided plan. Yet it is the teachers who are the professionals in this sphere of the school's internal daily life. It is highly desirable that the head and some teachers should be appointed a long time in advance and consulted on these questions, though they need not leave their present posts until the new school is ready. Alternatively, the teachers' organizations might set up their own panels of members specially interested in school organization. These panels could take professional advice, and should be consulted on the social and working implications of any new type of school building which might be proposed.

Curriculum and grouping

Because special interests and aptitudes develop as people grow up, a comprehensive school must offer a wide range of possible courses to meet the different needs of different pupils. No English comprehensive school is exactly like any other. Her Majesty's Inspectors of Schools may advise on curriculum and the internal organization of a school, but they cannot dictate; and almost all local education authorities give much freedom to the head of the school in such matters. No actual school, then, corresponds exactly to the description I am about to give. I have tried to present a reasonably accurate composite picture, conveying the essentials without blinding the reader with too much detail and countless qualifications.

An English comprehensive school normally provides a 'foundation course' of either two or three years (ages eleven to thirteen or fourteen) which is followed by all pupils. The usual subjects are: English, mathematics, history, geography, art, handcrafts (boys), housecraft (girls), physical education, music, science, and religion. Religion is the only subject in the curriculum which *must* be provided. French, or another second language, is sometimes studied by all pupils, more often by all except the less able. Latin is usually only begun by the more able pupils.

As children grow up, so their special aptitudes emerge more clearly. Pursuing its policy of giving an education suited to the needs of each pupil, the comprehensive school necessarily increases the number and character of different courses available to older pupils. This is done in two main stages. From thirteen or fourteen to sixteen the 'foundation' subjects are continued, but the time given to some of them is reduced, to others increased, to meet the special interests and needs of different children; and new subjects are introduced as required. The children begin to branch out in different directions, spreading wider as they grow to maturity. This kind of provision is well illustrated by the table on p. 99, showing the distribution of fourth-year pupils at a London school.[1]

Such provision exceeds in diversity anything a normal grammar or 'modern' school can offer.

The final stage, for those who remain, is from sixteen to eighteen or nineteen, called in England 'the sixth form'. Hitherto this stage of advanced study has been thought suitable only for that minority of boys and girls whose gifts are intellectual and academic. The comprehensive school certainly provides for them; but in addition it caters for the increasing number of other pupils – whose ability may vary from great to small – who seek the benefit of extended secondary education. The number of examination subjects available at this stage is commonly therefore much greater than that provided by the average grammar school. Many comprehensives schools offer twenty subjects or more. One school of 1,300 pupils includes such subjects as Russian, Spanish, Law, Accountancy, and Technical Drawing. But they also provide in various ways for the few who may have no examination qualifications or ambitions at all.

Streaming and non-streaming

'Put them all together and stream like mad' said a former Education Officer of the London County Council, Sir Graham Savage; and in the early days of comprehensive schools it was indeed almost universal practice to group children on the basis of general ability, in 'streams', as indicated by their performance in the eleven-plus examination or the reports from primary schools. Further and more

1. Reproduced from *London Comprehensive Schools*, p. 43.

Fourth-year forms		Third-year forms[1] 1	2	3	4	5	6	7	8	9	10	11	12	13	14	15	Total
4S	Science – Academic	14	12	3													29
K	Science – Academic		4	5	2	8	4	3	3	1							30
L	Languages – Academic	12	8		1			2									23
J	Commerce – Academic	1	6	5	6	7	1	2									28
G	General Arts – Academic		1	9	8		2	4	5								29
N	Engineering – boys		2	4	8	4	6	4	7								35
E	Practical – girls			3		4	1	3	2	3		1					17
T	Engineering					1	1	1	2	1	4	6	7	3	6		32
U	3 years to 'O' level							2	1	9	1	5	4			2	24
O	Commercial – girls				2	8	4	2	3	1	6	2	3				31
F	Commercial – boys				1		1	2	3	3	5	4	2	3	4	3	31
R	Catering			1	1		1		1	4	1	1	2	1	1	1	15
W	Woodwork								3		3	6		1	7	6	26
H	Horticulture						1	2		4	1	2		1			11
V	1 year – Vehicles							2	2	3	2	1	1	6	2		19
Z	1 year – Business				2		3	4		1	1	1	4	7	5	5	33
X	Christmas leavers						2	2			3	5	4	5	5	6	32
Y	Easter leavers						3		3	2	5	1	4	4	4	6	32

1. In each case, the numbering of the third-year form is a rough indication of comparative attainment at this stage.

accurate grouping according to ability in particular subjects, known as 'setting', was usually confined to those pupils already placed in the top third of their age group on general ability, and applied mainly in mathematics, science and languages. The constant re-arrangement of pupils in different groups which 'setting' entailed meant that it could only be used extensively in a big school with a lot of teachers.

There was much interest in the arrangements for transfer up and down between classes, and the first edition of this book (1963) went to some pains to give detailed tables showing how transfer actually worked. But since then research studies have supported the view that the whole principle of streaming, of which promotion and relegation are a necessary part, is unsound. For example, C. Lacey[1] has described the neuroses which afflicted twelve-year-old boys in the top stream of a grammar school; D. N. Holly[2] concludes that streaming discriminates in favour of middle-class and against working-class children; and Julienne Ford[3] finds that there is little mixing of children from different social classes in a streamed comprehensive school. So interest has moved to radically different forms of organization where what is seen as the palliative of a few individual transfers within a graded structure (which Monks has found to decline from five to seven per cent in the first year to around one per cent in the fourth year) has an insignificant place.

It is true that 'streaming' and to a lesser extent 'setting' still prevail in the majority of schools, but the picture is rapidly changing. Even the figures given by Monks from his 1965–6 survey[4] now appear to be quite out of date. In

1. *British Journal of Sociology*, vol. 17, no. 3, p. 245.
2. *ibid*, vol. 16, no. 2, p. 150.
3. *New Society*, 10 October 1968.
4. *op cit.*, pp. 45–6.

1968–9 I surveyed eighty-one schools, all established long enough to see at least one comprehensive intake right through the school, and all reasonably comprehensive in that not more than ten per cent of the children in their catchment area were 'lost' to local grammar or independent schools. Schools under the Inner London Education Authority were excluded, because of the difficulty of defining satisfactorily their degree of comprehensiveness. Otherwise the surveyed schools were widely distributed throughout England and Wales. No fewer than eleven of the eighty-one (fourteen per cent) were completely unstreamed in the first year, two in the second year, and one in the third year. These figures are, overall, two to three times greater than those given by Monks, and this after an interval of only three years. It must, however, be borne in mind that the Monks survey included a significant number of schools which were not truly comprehensive at all, and this may have diluted his figures.

I found, further, that four schools were unstreamed in most subjects in the first year, four in the second year, and two in the third year. Sixteen schools were unstreamed for a few subjects (other than physical education) in their first year, fourteen in the second year and fourteen in the third year.

Thus as many as thirty-one (thirty-eight per cent) of the eighty-one schools were operating in unstreamed situations to greater or lesser extent. One school was completely unstreamed for the first three years. This is the picture, remember, in the well-established comprehensive schools, with the rural areas well represented, which might be expected to be more conservative than many of the newcomers; though perhaps on the other hand, being confident of their success as pioneers, they are encouraged to go on reexamining old assumptions and re-building. Certainly a revolution of tremendous significance is quietly taking place.

Even where streaming continues it is usually in broad bands rather than in the fine differentiation of one class from another. Thus a school which takes in 300 new pupils aged eleven, who have to be divided into ten classes, may arrange them in these bands graded A, B and C according to ability, with three parallel forms in each of A and C, and four parallel forms in B. In the eighty-one schools surveyed, mixed ability classes within broad ability bands were favoured (for all or most subjects) by forty per cent in the first year, thirty-three per cent in the second year, and twenty-three per cent in the third year.

Mathematics was seen by head teachers as the subject presenting the greatest difficulty in the unstreamed class, and modern languages loomed almost as large. Science also caused some apprehension. At least three heads, however, felt that difficulties lie not with any particular subject but with the teacher. On the other hand one brave man against the tide queried whether a completely unstreamed class was really possible in any academic subject.

Why is such a fundamental change afoot? First, grouping by ability early in life tends to fix the expectation of teachers, and of children themselves, at that level – so development which might have taken place is instead restricted.[1] Secondly, a growing body of evidence indicates that better overall standards can be attained in the freer situation of the unstreamed group.[2]

I say 'can be attained' because the mere organizational act of putting children into classes of mixed ability will by

1. Two American educationalists, Lenore Jacobson and Robert Rosenthal (*Pygmalion in the Classroom*, Holt, Rinehart and Winston, 1968), named as late-developers in a San Francisco school children who were in fact chosen at random. The named children then blossomed – including a Mexican boy whose I.Q. rose from 61 to 106 in one year, and a girl whose I.Q. rose from 88 (indicating a slow learner) to 128 (indicating a gifted child).

2. *Grouping in Education*, ed. Yates (Wiley, 1966).

itself achieve nothing. Given support from the head and the goodwill of his colleagues, all then depends on the quality of the teacher. Under the leadership of a teacher who is confident, respected by the children, hardworking, good at planning ahead and a capable organizer of a wide range of different activities going on in the classroom (or outside it) at the same time, most impressive results can be achieved. In such a happy, busy, purposeful group individual talents flower in a manner rarely seen in more formal situations. On the other hand the unstreamed class in the charge of a teacher who lacks most of these qualities can be a disaster. There is no formal structure to ensure even a moderate degree of order and progress. It seems likely that the forthcoming report on the six-year N.F.E.R. research project on streaming in primary schools will reinforce this verdict.

It follows, then, that it would be unwise to dragoon teachers into adopting methods about which they do not feel confident or in which they do not believe. We must be content to persuade (and be persuaded), never to compel or impose. The best way of going about this reform is that which was so well demonstrated by John Walton when he was head of Beaminster School in Dorset. Walton, by his own enthusiasm and sincerity, generated a tremendous amount of interest and discussion concerning new approaches to education, not only among the staff but among parents and children too. The interest led to experiment by those who wished to experiment – but no one was compelled to join, and this meant that the changes which did take place were more likely to succeed and so attract those who had previously been doubtful.

Another pioneer of non-streaming is A. W. Rowe, whose principles were set out in a seminal book on English education.[1] Rowe's approach, first developed in 'modern' schools

1. *The Education of the Average Child* (Harrap, 1960).

and more recently applied in a large comprehensive school in Hull, demands tremendously thorough preparation of material by the teacher, and equally thorough forethought about how this material can be used effectively by the different individuals in his class. Learning will often take place singly or in groups, although there are occasions when the whole class is brought together and everyone's attention focussed on one topic. When you go into such a classroom you see first the people who matter – the children, busily concentrating on their particular jobs. Only then do you notice the teacher, quietly discussing a point with this child, or that group, moving around unobtrusively. How different from the dominant figure of old, declaiming on his dais at the front! Yet the change should not really surprise us. We take the more civilized methods for granted at the two extremes of our school system, in the infant school and the sixth form.

What we need, then, is flexibility in our grouping of children and in our teaching of them. The essential point is well made by Professor Tibble:

Unless we start . . . with the individual nature of the learning process and the varied needs of individual children, and relate our means and methods in a thoroughgoing way to this, we are producing but palliatives. It means placing the emphasis on learning not teaching, on the provision of incentives and occasions and materials for learning rather than on teaching methods and skills. The role and skill of the teacher is then not less important, but it is different, and certainly not less difficult. In Mr Rowe's words, 'he no longer imposes, he evokes'.[1]

However, Margaret Miles, a liberal head teacher does not see the issue in black and white terms. She wants children, unstreamed in the first year, to benefit from the experience of being members of different groups as they grow older, and suggests that these may well be based on common interests rather than on measured ability.[1]

Examination performances: the General Certificate of Education

One of the ways in which the success or failure of comprehensive schools can be judged objectively is by their record in the General Certificate of Education. Parents are naturally anxious lest reorganization of secondary schools on comprehensive lines will mean lower academic achievement by their children.

What are the facts, and what do they suggest?

First, let us be sure that we are making fair comparisons. Comprehensive schools are local education authority schools, an alternative to the system of separate grammar and 'modern' schools; it is only with this system that they should be compared, not with independent and direct grant schools.

In its annual statistics, the Department of Education and Science gives figures from which the performances in GCE of leavers from all maintained (LEA) schools during the school year can be calculated. It also gives details of the GCE performance of leavers from all the schools which are officially recognized as comprehensive, and these are much lower than the figures for LEA schools as a whole.

It is not generally realized, however, that the Department's figures make no attempt to distinguish between the GCE record of the majority of schools which have been comprehensive for at least seven years (and therefore have taken at least one group of children through a full secondary course) and the record of the majority, founded more recently, which are simply not old enough to have 'O' and 'A' level successes to set against the empty examination record of their 15-year-old leavers. Nor does the Department

1. *Comprehensive Schooling* (Longmans, 1968), p. 43.

try to distinguish between the GCE records of truly comprehensive schools on the one hand (those which take in a full range of ability at 11) and those schools which, though labelled 'comprehensive', in fact are 'creamed' – that is, lose a substantial proportion of the ablest children of their neighbourhood to selective grammar or independent schools.

During 1964–5, therefore, I made a modest pilot survey of GCE examination results in the earliest comprehensive schools – those which were founded, or assumed their present comprehensive character, between 1945 and 1955. This made possible a more rational comparison with the latest statistics from the Department of Education and Science then available, those for 1962–3.

From an eighty per cent return I found that twenty-four schools could reasonably be described as truly comprehensive in intake: that is, they recruited practically all local children, and any losses to grammar or independent schools did not exceed five per cent of the age-group. Almost all the schools were situated in rural areas of the north, midlands, and west, and none had any special cultural or material advantage. Indeed, the Department's regional figures show that these areas in general do less well in examinations than do those of the prosperous south, south-east, and south-west. One reason for this is that the professional, middle-class element is under-represented in the social composition of the former group.

The comparative figures, expressed in percentages, were:

1962–3	GCE 'O' level passes		GCE 'A' level passes
	1 or more	5 or more	2 or more
All maintained (LEA) schools in England and Wales	26	13	5.3
24 early comprehensive schools (3,610 leavers)	32	16	7.5

In 1968–9 I made a similar survey of comprehensive schools throughout England and Wales (other than those of the Inner London Education Authority, whose degree of comprehensiveness was difficult to determine) which had been established as comprehensives for at least seven years, and which did not lose more than ten per cent of the children residing in their catchment area to local grammar or independent schools.

Of 151 non-London schools listed in the previous edition of this book as being 'broadly comprehensive' and established in or before 1961 (Leicestershire high schools 1964), returns were received from 110, or seventy-three per cent. This was a good response to a private inquiry, particularly at a time when head teachers are under serious strain from the many demands being made of them by research workers in addition to their heavy regular administrative duties. I wish to express my appreciation of their generous help (some returns had to be completed late in the evenings or on Saturday afternoons) and at the same time to urge that all schools be given much more administrative help than they have at present. The provision of such information as this is essential in a developing system, but it ought not to entail the personal sacrifice which it does at present.

Of the 110 schools which replied, 82 (75 per cent) had a truly comprehensive intake as defined above, but fourteen of these were Leicestershire high schools which obviously had no GCE examination results to report, and one 11–18 school, while completing the rest of the questionnaire, was unable to provide examination figures. This left sixty-eight schools out of ninety-six 11–18 schools (seventy-one per cent) which were truly comprehensive, and sixty-seven schools giving GCE results.

The sixty-seven schools were distributed widely throughout England and Wales (except inner London) and ranged from small rural schools to big schools of 2,000 pupils on working-class housing estates. Forty-one were situated in country towns (twenty-two of them in Wales) and the remaining twenty-six in cities, suburbs and industrial conurbations. The second group is smaller because it is in these areas that grammar school competition still takes its toll of the nominally comprehensive schools.

Overall figures are a better index in these matters than is the attempted comparison of individual schools or small groups of schools, where there are too many special factors to permit of proper 'controls'. The broad picture drawn from large numbers is that relied upon by the Department of Education and Science to bring out regional differences.

Two of these sixty-seven schools were in the Isle of Man, which is not covered by DES returns. Of the remaining sixty-five, twenty-four were in Wales, where 'O' level results are above the national average, 'A' level slightly below it; eleven in the more favoured regions where both 'O' and 'A' level results are above the national average (South-West 8, South-East 2, Greater London 1); and no fewer than thirty in 'educationally disadvantaged' regions where both 'O' and 'A' level results are below the national average (West Midlands 12, Yorkshire and Humberside 7, Northern 6, North-West 4, East Midlands 1).

In the light of this distribution, there is no reason to suppose that the latest figures are unduly optimistic; indeed they are likely to improve when the south-east and Greater London achieve more genuine comprehensive schools and make their proper contribution.

The examination record, expressed in percentages, was as follows:

1967–8	GCE 'O' level passes (including CSE grade 1 as equivalent)		GCE 'A' level passes
	1 or more	5 or more	2 or more
67 established comprehensive schools (12,493 leavers)	39.4	20.1	9.7

By the time this book is published the examination results for all maintained schools (still mainly 'modern' and grammar) in 1967–8 should be known, and the curious reader will be able to make his own comparisons. This, however is not the most important aspect – though we may confidently expect that the established comprehensive schools will be seen at least to be holding their own in the light of any such exercise, and this may assuage the doubts of those who still fear for our academic standards.

The first of two important facts is that in five years examination performances by pupils in comprehensive schools has improved by from twenty-two to twenty-five per cent at 'O' level and twenty-nine per cent at 'A' level; and these figures are based on a larger number of schools and school leavers than were the earlier ones, which were themselves impressive at the time. With the extension of comprehensive schooling the demand for more places in higher education is going to be intensified.

Secondly, as appears from other aspects of the survey dealt with elsewhere in this chapter, this advance in scholastic achievement, measured in the traditional way, has gone hand in hand with a significant move *away* from those pressures which have been hitherto generally thought necessary to keep children working at full stretch: streaming, competitive marks and prizes, and traditional forms of punishment. It would be wrong to assume that the schools which have markedly relaxed their competitive incentives in favour of a more cooperative and confidence-giving atmosphere have been more successful than those which have moved much less in this direction; there is no such evidence. One may legitimately observe, however, that nearly forty per cent of the surveyed schools are experimenting with non-streaming for younger children, and that such attitudes are bound to influence the climate of the school as a whole. Here are the first signs of what, if it developed, would be a change of fundamental importance: a shift from competitive learning to co-operative learning.

An interesting example of the way the academic work of the comprehensive schools has developed is to be found at Mellow Lane, just under 1,000 strong, which serves the industrial area of Hayes in Middlesex. Though still subject to grammar school competition it has attained parity of esteem by its own efforts. Though founded in 1948 it did not receive its first group of selected children until 1950, when only two out of fifty parents named Mellow Lane among the three grammar school choices open to them. Today it can fill its proportion of 'selected' pupils from first choices. There are 45–50 'selected' pupils entering each year, but well over 130 candidates for CSE, over 100 for GCE 'O' level and 40–50 for 'A' level. Some 25–30 proceed to universities, colleges of education, polytechnics or art colleges.

In the north of England Colne Valley High School has 1,500 boys and girls. Out of 53 students who left in 1968 after at least two years in the sixth form, eighteen went to degree courses, seventeen to colleges of education, nine to other full-time courses, and nine into employment.

In Wales Ysgol Y Preseli, Crymych, has 600 boys and girls. Twenty-nine sat 'A' level in 1968 and gathered ten distinctions, plus two further distinctions at scholarship level. In the little Ysgol Maes Garmon at Mold, in 1967 thirty children (eight of whom had failed the eleven-plus) sat 'O' level and averaged eight passes per pupil, with a substantial number of passes at grades one and two.

Sir William Romney's School at Tetbury in Gloucestershire has only 450 pupils and a sixth form of only nineteen. Two children out of three have unskilled or semi-skilled parents, and not more than two per cent come from professional homes. Despite its small size, with a normal staff ratio Sir William Romney's offers a reasonable choice of subjects, and in 1968 twenty-six 'A' level papers were taken with the following results: three grade A, eight grade B, two grade C, five grade D, five grade E, two grade O, one fail. Fifteen ex-pupils went on to full-time courses in higher education at colleges of music, art, teacher training, a polytechnic, and universities.

Finally, on the Kirkby Estate already described, St Kevin's School takes all the Roman Catholic boys from Kirkby and a new overspill settlement. In 1966 there were nine pupils in the sixth form; today there are 100, and in 1968 eleven pupils went to universities, eight to colleges of education.

Such achievements are most praiseworthy. Straining after examination results in a fierce competition for places at universities and other places of higher education, however, has no appeal for these schools or for supporters of comprehensive education in general. Their aim is sound, unhurried growth in which the normal challenges of the environment are met and overcome, not the forcing of the hothouse to which the pressures of GCE have now become akin. We must look forward to the day when the more sensitive and enlightened approach to CSE replaces GCE certainly at 'O' and possibly at 'A' level. We must also ensure that appropriate courses in higher education are available for all who need them so that, just as primary schools are finding their souls with the gradual disappearance of the eleven-plus, so all secondary schools can devote themselves wholeheartedly to providing, at an appropriate pace, for the different needs of all their pupils.

Eleven-plus 'failures'

It is no longer necessary to amass examples of children who fail to get to a grammar school at eleven and later make good. The serious weaknesses of selection at eleven are now accepted.

Nevertheless we must not forget that this selection process is still going on, and that it has very serious consequences for individual people. Ministers and chief education officers may take a grand view twenty years ahead, but this is little help to the child of eleven in an area not yet re-organized. When I mention the following random examples of late development in a few comprehensive schools, I really have in mind the army of nameless ones who could have come up likewise, but have been lost in the quicksands of our selective system.

In a Home Counties school, four of the five university places obtained in 1961 were won by boys who had failed the eleven-plus, and one of these won a State scholarship. The head of the same school said:

I have identical twins in the school, one of whom failed and one who passed the eleven-plus. Both are now in a 'grammar' form and occupy second and third positions respectively.

At Bristol, seventeen comprehensive school pupils who had failed the eleven-plus secured twenty-six advanced level passes among them. Six of them were accepted by universities, including one at Cambridge.

Elsewhere the examples of late development in comprehensive schools abound: John, whose I.Q. was 91, gaining five GCE passes at ordinary level: Jack, I.Q. 103, gaining six passes; Jean, an eleven-plus failure who gained eight ordinary-level passes before taking three advanced level science subjects; James, who had failed to get into not only a grammar school but a central (intermediate) school, gaining six passes; Andrew, who came from the bottom stream of central school, passing advanced-level GCE in history and mathematics, adding economics later, and now at a university; David, an eleven-plus failure, going on to win a Trevelyan Scholarship at Christ Church, Oxford. A report by the Inner London Education Authority gives several interesting case-histories, and in particular lists nine boys who left Peckham Manor School in 1966. All nine had been given I.Q.s below that usually required for entry to grammar schools at eleven plus, but all went to universities.[1]

It would be tedious to go on. There is overwhelming evidence that the comprehensive schools are giving justice, in so far as that is possible, to children whose early progress has been held back. And yet ... how far there is to go! The head of one comprehensive school in the west, himself a distinguished university scholar and educationist, says:

After extensive inquiries, I have not found any pupil who failed the eleven-plus who has overcome his sense of inferiority at this failure, irrespective of his performance even at university level.

If that is so with exceptions who fight their way back, how much deeper is the humiliation of those who, because comprehensive reform is far from completed, must for ever accept that early stamp: 'Inferior quality – reject.' It is specious to argue that all have the chance to reverse an adverse verdict at eleven-plus. The selective system is so constructed that only a minority of children can ever join the elect; there must always be a majority who are cast out.

The worry and tension created in so many homes before

1. *London Comprehensive Schools 1966*, pp. 97–101.

the examination are harmful enough. The after-effects of failure are very much worse. They are obvious when one member of a family succeeds and another fails. They are, however, just as hurtful to any child who is dismissed as unworthy – and despite all the plausible arguments in favour of selection, that is how children and parents see it.

Those who are most deeply hurt usually assume a poker face to hide the wound. It is not healed in a matter of months or even years. Many young people react by revolting against the society which has spurned them. Crime mounts every year. Adolescents are punished for seemingly senseless acts of destruction, with no noticeable effect. The hidden offenders, however, are ourselves – we who tolerate the leisured and incomplete reform of social and educational policies both cruel and futile, if more refined than the things in *Oliver Twist* and *The Water Babies* which now horrify us.

The various churches profess to follow a teacher who fiercely attacked all such distinctions damaging to human dignity. Today they are worried because many people, though still persisting that they are Christians, have lost faith in the leadership of clergymen; yet each as a body has done little about our own form of *apartheid*, the compulsory segregation of young children in different types of school. Here is a social evil which the Christian church ought not to tolerate for a moment.

Although there is no concerted action, some clergy are very conscious of the basic flaws in our society. Writing with rare insight in an article about Oxford-Borstal camps, the Rev. J. N. Jory put his finger on the essential point:

We are always giving each other labels, categorizing, classifying and then thinking that we have simplified our problem, that we know where we stand. In creating such categories we only deceive ourselves, and sometimes hinder those who strive to live happy and purposeful lives. God made people, we have often sought to label them. . . .

We changed the word delinquency to need. The need of every boy to know that he 'belonged' to somebody, that decency and happiness are bound up together. . . . Need so many-sided that it spells poverty. We cannot expect penitence in those who look back in anger, and we ought to ask ourselves: 'Is the poverty of the age due to my greed, my blindness, my with-holding?' . . .

The restoration of self-respect, essential to every offender who has been humiliated by our society and yet seeks to live a life of dignity and decency, can only come through other people; people willing to accept him, have confidence in him and give him the opportunity to express himself.[1]

I have stressed here the human wrong done by com-pulsory segregation at eleven-plus, because that is by far the most important consideration. Those who harden their hearts, however, may possibly be convinced by the ma-terial aspect, by the need to use every person's talent to its fullest capacity. That depends on everyone feeling that he counts, and that he is capable of doing important work which is valued by others. It also requires us to pursue a policy of full opportunity and encouragement in schools, instead of restricted opportunity and discouragement, which is still all too common. All who are concerned about national output and the quality of British workmanship should consider very hard whether the shortcomings they deplore do not have their origins in a school system which has automatically dashed the self-respect of the majority of children, and for some has destroyed it.

Less able children

Examinations, of course, are by no means confined to GCE. I have concentrated on that because it is a standard

1. *Yorkshire Post*, 13 July 1961.

nationally accepted and understood outside schools, and the only one in which objective comparisons can be made between the records of different types of school.

In fact the comprehensive schools run a wide range of courses for children of around average ability, such as those shown in the earlier table of fourth-year work at a London school.

In 1965 a new Certificate of Secondary Education was introduced. It was intended for children who were thought to be below GCE standard, but grade one of CSE is now recognized as equivalent to GCE 'O' level. Many hope that CSE, a teacher-controlled examination based on children's needs rather than on external syllabuses, will before long replace the GCE 'O' level altogether.

It was originally assumed that the top twenty per cent of an age-group would take GCE, and that the new lower certificate would cater for the next forty per cent, leaving a bottom forty per cent for whom any examination was considered undesirable. However, the figures given earlier suggest that thirty to fifty per cent will attempt GCE, and that rising standards may encourage perhaps another thirty per cent from those in the lower band to attempt the new CSE in individual subjects at least.

The large size of many comprehensive schools enables them to make much-needed special provision for backward children. Specially trained teachers are appointed – when they can be found. Backward children are commonly grouped in small classes under such teachers, and not taught by subject specialists. The school's aim is not to detach the backward child from a normal environment for his whole school life, but to help him to master the basic skills of reading and number, to dispel emotional blocks, and to fit him to resume his place in a normal class at the earliest possible moment. Some schools prefer to leave the backward child in a normal class and withdraw him only for special tuition during certain periods.

While quite a lot is being done in remedial teaching, provision for psychological guidance is less satisfactory. It is right that we should expect our teachers to be more than mere classroom specialists, that they should care for the general welfare of their pupils. But in a disturbed society such as ours, with divorce and movement from one community to another as commonplaces, there are great emotional stresses on many children. We need here to follow America, as in so many other matters, by establishing guidance departments headed by trained people in every large secondary school, or alternatively in area groups of junior and senior high schools.

Four Institutes of Education (Keele, Reading, Swansea and Exeter) now, in fact, train experienced graduate and non-graduate teachers to become school counsellors; and a few progressive local education authorities are appointing them to suitable posts. Thus Longslade School in Leicestershire has three trained school counsellors, two of whom are deputy heads.

Children's attitudes

How attractive and worthwhile does the comprehensive school seem to the pupils? Despite being, as Napoleon said, 'a nation of shopkeepers', we are too patriarchal really to accept that the customer is always right. So it has been left to an Australian, Dr T. W. G. Miller, to investigate pupils' attitudes and consider the question of values from their point of view.[1]

Miller's study related to boys aged thirteen to fourteen. In three different parts of England he compared the attitudes of boys in grammar schools on certain matters with those of boys in comprehensive schools (termed 'comprehensive grammar' below) whose abilities and home

1. *Values in the Comprehensive School* (Oliver and Boyd, 1961).

backgrounds were similar. He likewise compared similar groups in 'modern' and comprehensive schools ('comprehensive modern' below). His most significant conclusions were these:

1. The 'comprehensive grammar' boys had a very slightly higher proportion of active leisure-time interests (e.g. playing rather than watching football) than the boys from separate grammar schools. Third came the 'comprehensive modern' groups, a bad last those from 'modern' schools.

2. The group which had the highest opinion of its own school was 'comprehensive modern'; second came 'comprehensive grammar', third grammar school, fourth 'modern' school. At the same time the boys' estimate of their school's standing in the eyes of the public was realistic: 1. grammar school; 2. comprehensive school; 3. 'modern' school.

3. 'Comprehensive grammar' and 'comprehensive modern' together had the highest opinion of the courses offered by their schools. Grammar school and 'modern' school came lower, and close together.

4. Tests of 'morale' and attitudes to schooling and education generally (e.g. homework) produced this order: 1. 'comprehensive grammar' closely followed by grammar school – the difference was scarcely significant; 3. 'comprehensive modern'; 4. 'modern' school.

5. Finally, all the boys were asked: 'Do you wish to leave school as soon as possible?' The answer 'No' came as follows: 'comprehensive grammar' ninety-three per cent; grammar school eighty-three per cent; 'comprehensive modern' seventy-two per cent; 'modern' school fifty-seven per cent.

Miller's work shows very clearly that the comprehensive schools are already meeting pupils' needs which in a divided secondary system are generally unsatisfied. It further shows that they are encouraging a bigger proportion to stay longer at school, learning to use their talents to the full. One of the most significant features of his findings is that even in the 'modern' schools, where pupils clearly felt themselves and the school to be inferior, more than half wanted to continue their education. There is an enormous unsatisfied demand for higher secondary education: a significant reserve of talent thirsting for full nourishment and training. Crowther found that two out of five of our ablest boys leave school by the age of sixteen. This situation must be remedied.

Against this favourable picture, however, must be set the query raised tentatively by Douglas, Ross and Simpson, who found that markedly fewer fifteen-year-old pupils of high ability in comprehensive schools, compared with their peers in grammar schools, wished to continue with full-time education after leaving school.[1] And Julienne Ford has found that within a streamed comprehensive school social class divisions are as pronounced as they were under the old system. Friendship patterns are similar, the employment horizons of working class children no wider; and this despite a house system with good accommodation and facilities.[2]

Staying on at school

The Ministry of Education's published statistics do not show the proportions of each age group who stay at school for a full fifth, sixth, or seventh year. However, from the numbers given for different ages it is possible to make rough calculations. In January 1967 about forty per cent of their respective age-groups (in maintained schools only) would complete a fifth year, twenty-three per cent a sixth year, and eleven per cent a seventh year.[3]

What is the position in comprehensive schools? Naturally

1. *All Our Future*, p. 63.
2. loc. cit.
3. *Statistics of Education*, 1967 vol. 1, Table 7, shows that 47% of the relevant age-group stayed at school to the age of 15, 27% to 16, 15% to 17, 6% to 18.

there is a good deal of variation, depending partly on the sort of local society served by the school, partly on how long the school has been in existence, and partly on how far it is 'creamed' by grammar and independent schools. During 1968–9 returns from comprehensive schools showed that from half to two thirds of their pupils commonly stayed for a fifth year, between twenty and thirty per cent normally stayed for a sixth year, and between fifteen and twenty per cent normally stayed for a seventh year. In each case certain schools were achieving much higher proportions, while other schools, growing from former 'modern' or central schools or situated in poor districts, have much lower figures.

The general picture, as one might expect, is similar to that given by my survey of examination results, and is confirmed in London.[1] More young people are staying on in comprehensive schools at each stage, and particularly at sixth form level, than was the case seven years ago. This is, however, part of a general trend as the value of an extended education is increasingly being appreciated by society as a whole.

There are two possible reasons why pupils are staying rather longer at comprehensive schools. One is simply that these schools offer a more efficient service. They provide more courses. Late developers, too, who would otherwise be sent at eleven to a 'modern' school with perhaps no GCE or other examination courses, are able to move up to the examination forms quite easily.

The other possibility is that the school itself may be a more attractive society to live in than is the average 'modern' school or even a selective grammar school. Miller's findings suggest that this is true also. But if it is so, why? Are the teaching methods very different from those practised in grammar and/or 'modern' schools? Are the

1. *London Comprehensive Schools 1966*, pp. 101–3.

incentives to learning more attractive, or the deterrents to laziness and misbehaviour more effective? What sort of a society is it to live in?

Reform of the curriculum and teaching methods

The new thinking in education could not for long be confined to organization. During the past five years major changes have been introduced in the field of curriculum and methods of teaching. Comprehensive schools have taken an active part in these developments, though they have by no means monopolized them; and as a result they have become more interesting and purposeful places in which to teach and to learn.

The main agents of reform here have been the Schools Council – a body staffed mainly by the Department of Education and Science, financed by local education authorities, and controlled (policy-wise) by teachers – and the Nuffield Foundation. From both have come substantial grants of money to finance large-scale investigations and experiments. Other interested groups have contributed their expertise – for example the Area Training Organizations (better known as Institutes of Education) which bring together all the parties in a region which are substantially involved in the education of teachers: local education authorities, teachers' associations, colleges of education, universities, and the Department of Education and Science.

Fundamentally the aim has been to bring syllabuses up to date and to make them relevant to all children. Hitherto we have relied on the blotting-paper memory of most selected children to take in and then, at the appropriate examination, to regurgitate the facts and second-hand thoughts we fed them with. That is no longer acceptable in a comprehensive school which is providing in a flexible way for all kinds of ability. So what is taught in science, mathematics, the humanities, languages, and so on, is getting a radical overhaul.

Clearly the overhaul must also embrace methods of teaching these subjects. One new development, which harnesses technology to the special needs of the individual student, is programmed learning. Another is the language laboratory. A third is 'team teaching', which means that a group of teachers variously qualified pool their skills and knowledge to undertake a programme of work, usually disregarding the usual subject boundaries, with several classes of children who are themselves put into one large group. Perhaps a hundred children will meet in a lecture theatre to hear a lecture or watch a film; then they will be divided so that groups of various size, or single individuals, can work on appropriate aspects of the programme. Thus (for example) in a project on archaeology forty of the hundred may, after careful preparation, be out of school visiting a local site, several smaller groups may be drawing plans in the history room or developing photographs in a laboratory, while three or four scholarly individuals may be translating Latin inscriptions in the library.

Inevitably the revolution is in full swing only, so far, in a minority of comprehensive schools and among a minority of their teachers. The great majority of comprehensive school teachers are themselves products of grammar schools who learned by traditional methods, and who have since taught in either grammar or 'modern' schools. Even the young teachers fresh from college or university may be illprepared for the new methods; for the training of teachers itself needs a wind of change. Nevertheless, change in the content and methods of education is afoot, and proceeding apace.

2. THE SCHOOL AS A SOCIETY AND IN SOCIETY

The headmaster

L'état, c'est moi. One of the sharpest differences I have noticed between schools in England and those across the Atlantic is that in the status and role of the headmaster (and headmistress). Over there it is felt that the school belongs to the local community, which has a real say in what goes on. The head has an important part to play, but he is still just one of the team.

In England it is quite different, though a real change seems at last to be beginning. The head (I speak of all types of school) is king of the castle, and any discussions parents may have with him on the running of the school are by grace and favour, not as of right. We have to contend with two kinds of autocracy: that of the local authority, which decides in its wisdom which type of school a child should go to, and that of the headmaster.

Even when, as is beginning to happen a little more, parents are given an effective say about the kind of school most suitable for their child, their participation too often ends at the school door. It is far from unusual for a child to be put into one course or denied admission to another without reference to the parents. In the late seventeenth century Dr Busby, headmaster of Westminster, refused to remove his hat when King Charles II visited the school lest his pupils should suspect that there was any man greater than himself. That tradition has persisted. 'I mean to be boss in my own school' is a familiar phrase. But is it 'his' school?

This does not mean that head teachers in general are lacking in concern for their pupils' welfare: not at all. They are, if anything, too possessive, too impatient of the parents' views, so sure that they know best that they prefer where possible to take unilateral action. It is true that they proclaim, with one voice, that a parent can always come to see them about his child; but not infrequently a parent's doubts really turn on aspects of the school's organization, attitudes, and methods which require general appraisal before the individual case can be fully understood. There are parents' evenings, open days, and so on; but full, free, organized discussion of the fundamental principles and practices on which the school stands is as rare as snow in summer. It *can* happen; how rarely it does!

This is the background against which we must view the head of the English comprehensive school today. One must not expect a revolution overnight. Changing a framework is one thing, changing attitudes of mind quite another. What we see, in fact, is an impressive concern for the individual child. The fear that a comprehensive-school head must be a remote impersonal figure is not borne out. Indeed, in some ways he is better able to interest himself in people than can heads of smaller schools. But his rule, though always benevolent, is still paternal.

To some extent this stems from the organization of the large school. Coventry's pattern of various buildings, grouped on a common campus, seems to embody the basic concept of the English comprehensive school – diversity within a greater unity. It also calls for a larger view of the role of the head – a view familiar to us, in fact, in the bigger 'public' schools. The head becomes a kind of prime minister, *primus inter pares*, working closely with a band of responsible senior colleagues – heads of houses and/or of lower and upper schools, and heads of departments.

He is – or ought to be – assisted by an administrative staff which is under an officer of experience and personal quality, a man or woman capable of assuming major responsibilities. This is one of London's many contributions to

English school organization, though it is of course already common in America.

It would be petty and inefficient if the headmaster attempted the detailed running of the school, as the head of a small school has to do. His concern is at once larger and more intimate, and may be classified under the three Ps: (1) policy and planning; (2) public relations outside the school – particularly important in a school which is, or should be, *par excellence*, a school for the community; (3) personal relations inside the school. Relief from administrative chores frees the head to use his special personal qualities in making direct contact with all the staff and for contacts with some pupils too – for example in societies, the school council, and an occasional lesson. At the top, therefore, the comprehensive school needs precisely the kind of democratic leadership, warm, wise, and balanced, which is needed at the helm of a college, a university, or a boarding school.

All this is fine in theory. The critics, however, have repeatedly suggested that there are not enough teachers capable of doing this job well. Sir Edward Boyle, for example, said in 1959: 'It is the Government's view, and I am sure this is right, that only the very exceptional head teacher can infuse a spirit of unity into a school of say 2,000 pupils.'[1] This view may arise in part from the discredited but persistent belief that the pool of ability is small and limited. More important, however, is the fact that in most comprehensive schools the administrative staff is completely inadequate in both numbers and status, so that the head is tied to his desk. He is unable to do the job which he not only wants to do but was in theory appointed to do.

Judgement in such matters must always be personal, so no case can be proved one way or the other. If my own

1. *Education*, 23 January 1959, p. 154.

comment is worth anything, it is only because over the years my work has brought me into contact with a large number of teachers and administrators in schools, universities, and colleges, including many headmasters and headmistresses. Where one is taken for granted and, like Father Brown's postman, an ordinary person calling for no special show, an accurate opinion is perhaps more likely to be formed.

In 1954 I wrote of one small comprehensive school and its headmaster:

It must not be thought that Castle Rushen is extremely 'progressive' . . . Its virtues are the virtues of moderation, balance, and a liberal attitude of mind. Mr Cretney prefers leading by the hand to pushing and pulling; example to exhortation . . . In his care to hasten slowly he has introduced some [traditional] practices which will be difficult to uproot. But it must be conceded that they are largely compensated by personal attention to every child.[1]

Of course, all headmasters and headmistresses have different qualities. Nevertheless my overall picture of comprehensive-school heads comes increasingly near to that description. They are sincere, devoted men and women, aware of detail and of individuals in their schools, but not to the exclusion of wider ideas. They are not much interested in publicity. Fortunately, however, head teachers are now beginning to publish their own accounts of their aims and experiences, which will be invaluable both immediately and for the future historian of education.

The staff

These heads, whose general calibre is impressive, are drawn largely from the ranks of teachers who have served in separate types of school. Younger men and women are now appearing, however, whose liberal sympathies and

1. *Education*, 7 May 1954, pp. 791–2.

administrative gifts have taken them into responsible posts in comprehensive and similar schools. Behind them throng many good candidates.

The real problem is not finding enough good heads, but ensuring a satisfying, sufficiently responsible position for the many who are capable of being good heads but who will never get the opportunity. As schools – all types of schools – get bigger, and more teachers are recruited, the chances of promotion to headships get less. If we stick to rat-race rules, we shall have fierce competition for the top posts, possibly distorting the values of assistant teachers, disturbing the harmony of what should be a happy co-operating community, and producing a growing number of dispirited men who count themselves failures.

A staff of thirty to a hundred teachers is a body of unusually gifted people. All are important, and it is necessary that all should feel important (in a responsible, not vain, sense) if they are to give of their best. What happens now?

In the big comprehensive school there is usually a hierarchy of senior members of staff. The headmaster has his cabinet of deputies, heads of houses and heads of departments. Outside the magic circle are the other assistant teachers, who have little direct say in policy. It is true that periodic staff meetings are usually held, and that questions of major policy may be discussed there. There are also meetings of house staff and department staff, to consider detailed matters affecting those sections; and a good school will also have its senior-commonroom committee, elected regardless of official status. But a large meeting is a poor substitute for a round-table gathering when thrashing out the finer points of some important issue; and transmission of one's point of view through a head of department is uncertain, unsatisfying, and liable to lose much of its conviction when conveyed (if it is properly conveyed) at second hand.

The fault mainly lies in the promotion ladder built up by successive Burnham reports: a series of graded posts for which teachers must compete, which has caused hard feelings and bad relations in many staff rooms. This system puts a premium on ability to organize, whereas one might have thought that ability to teach was the most precious quality of all.

What we need in schools is a recognition that all members of staff are doing work so important that financial differentiation between them *on the basis of work as such* cannot reasonably be made. Experience, which all acquire as the years go by, is a different matter. and can be fairly assessed. So can extra years of training and higher qualifications, which one would wish to encourage.

There is much to be said for an academic community which rates classroom teaching as high as anything else, and passes round the administrative jobs in turn, so that in due course all experience and benefit from a share in the inner councils. Some may appear at first sight less suited to this than others; but people do tend to grow with the job. Human beings are adaptable, as educationists should be the first to recognize. Capacity to learn is not confined to the pupils. The larger benefits to the happiness and unity of the staff could be immense.

Democracy in school

I have observed that the teachers in our comprehensive schools are themselves the products of grammar schools, and that their experience has usually been in grammar or 'modern' schools. It is not surprising, then, to find that apart from the quite limited belief that secondary-school children should not be segregated in separate types of school, these teachers at first transplanted into the new schools almost all the standard grammar-school attitudes to children's education.

Take, for example, prefects: an élite of older children, who help in the running of the school and the control of other pupils. I am not one of those who believe that children do not need the guiding hand of authority at all; far from it. The business of education is fundamentally that of gradually changing the helpless immature baby, completely dependent on adult authority, into the capable, mature, free adult. It is a long process. Control eventually gives way to guidance, guidance gives way to advice; and conversely the growing child assumes increasing responsibilities for both himself and others. It is right that older pupils should take an increasing share in the internal government of the school. But the need and the right to have this experience belong to *all* children at the appropriate point for their social group, not just to a select few.

Conservative-minded critics think this concern for education in social democracy is irrelevant to the purpose of the comprehensive school. H. C. Dent, for example, wrote:

One thing at a time. The comprehensive principle itself offers a sufficiently large, difficult, and exciting field for experiment; do not further complicate the task of those who are adventuring in it by including elements which, however attractive, are essentially extraneous.[1]

In fact this business of selecting and elevating a few, rejecting and excluding the mass, is at least as important in a school's social life as in the classroom. It goes to the heart of our education and social philosophy; and there is now evidence that this is increasingly being appreciated by teachers. Seven years ago I found that ninety-six per cent of the first comprehensive schools had prefects; today the figure is down to eighty-one per cent. More important, though the name remains, in several schools it does not

1. Essay in *Comprehensive Schools Today* (Councils and Education Press, 1955), p. 40.

involve the selection of an élite because all members of one year-group are regarded as prefects. In two schools the sixth form is not involved at all, but leaves it to the fifth. The aim is to spread responsibility very widely through the school.

These are examples of the moderate, liberal, far-sighted policy to which I referred earlier. The old trappings remain; but within, new growth and fresh ideas are slowly and quietly beginning to transform the scene.

Seven years ago few had a School Council elected by some or all of the children; today, thirty-six per cent have either a School Council or House Councils. Sometimes the elected children learn to administer money wisely – an excellent experience. There is much to be said for giving the older pupils, at least, training in democratic procedures and responsibilities in this way, and nothing serious to be said against it. If we want more people to vote and take part in local government, we must acknowledge that participation in the running of the affairs of one's school is an important preparation.

Though changes in this area of school life are evidence that questions are being asked and ideas are thriving, it is probably still true to say that as a body today's comprehensive schools vary from moderately conservative to cautiously liberal, with flashes of radicalism here and there. Their attitude to the wearing of school uniform is typical of much else. Practically all have a school uniform; on the other hand, though all are encouraged to wear it, the policy is applied with sympathy and tolerance. Upper-school girls often have considerable latitude, with some individual choice of style or colour. At least one school allows the older girls to wear make-up, and all girls to wear jewellery in moderation.

It is possible that much of the outrageous make-up and dress flaunted by teenagers is produced by the need to revolt against authoritarian school standards. Might it not be better if more schools did what a few already do – deal with personal health, beauty, taste, and design in an appropriate part of the curriculum? Magazines like *Which?* have begun to educate the middle-class adult, to rescue him from the domination of commercial advertising. But only the schools, and I think particularly the comprehensive schools, can teach the whole nation that self-determination in this matter is both possible and desirable.

Limited freedom in an approved area can be most frustrating. We are so often saying: 'Do what you like, apart from the thing you most want to do.' Young men and women can only become free by practising freedom. I have already said that they are not yet ready for complete freedom; but I believe that this area, of dress and personal appearance, is one for which they *are* ready, one which concerns most of them enormously, and which we should use to ease the gradual transition of responsibility to their own shoulders. They must bear it all very very soon. On such matters as dress, taste, and etiquette we can move earlier into our future role of friendly advisers.

Incentives

The picture is one of much more positive change when we turn to incentives in the surveyed comprehensive schools. Seven years ago, eighty-nine per cent gave their children ranking orders in class, either overall positions (1st, 5th, 30th, and so on) or positions for particular subjects only. Today that proportion has dropped dramatically to fifty-four per cent; and several of these schools maintain the practice only in the first two or three years.

The award of prizes or trophies, however, is still widely practised: seventy-four per cent (eighty-seven seven years ago) give them for academic work; eighty-one per cent (eighty-nine) for games and athletics; and seventy-five per cent (eighty-five) for other achievements or contributions to the life of the school community. About five per cent of the schools, as before, do not make any such awards.

There are still, then, carrots to dangle in front of the noses of the most eager. But what of the stubborn laggards? They have fallen so far behind that the carrots are too far out of reach to have any appeal. In the last resort most schools still fall back on the whip (in fact, the cane) – but it is used very rarely, and by twenty-two per cent of the schools never. A headmaster who admitted to caning sometimes once said: 'I dislike it more than ever as a method of punishment'. Another said: 'I doubt its efficiency, and do not now use it.' Professor E. B. Castle, at one time headmaster of the Quaker boarding school at Leighton Park, Reading, has written that his became an infinitely better school when he finally laid aside his cane.[1] But against this liberal trend we cannot forget that the comprehensive school suffered its biggest reverse when Risinghall, the school which had abandoned corporal punishment in one of the toughest districts one could find, was closed.[2]

Detention, either after school or during the dinner hour, is still the most common form of punishment, but enthusiasm for it has declined; and the same is true of such devices as old-fashioned 'impositions', order and conduct marks, report cards, and exclusion from normal routine or privileges. One senses that where they remain it is very much a case of *faute de mieux*. Some four per cent of the schools have practically no official forms of punishment.

Of the picture seven years ago I wrote: 'a striking feature is the extent to which schools deal with children (even in "the last resort") on their own, rather than consulting the parents', and I hoped for some significant change in perhaps twenty years' time. In fact – and this is a further

1. *People in School* (Heinemann, 1953), p. 23.
2. See chapter 4.

indication that we are living in a revolutionary period in education – that transformed situation is already with us. No fewer than twenty-eight per cent of the heads say that they frequently consult parents about their children's behaviour, either by letter or by interview; and another fifty per cent do so occasionally. This is a powerful indication of the extent to which the job of education has come to be recognized as a partnership between home and school, even though the consultation is mainly about individual pupils rather than general principles.

There is still, of course, a lot of room for improvement in the schools of England as a whole. Look at the eager faces in the early years of the primary schools; then look at the rows of reluctant fourteen-year-olds in the less liberal secondary schools of all types. What have we done to them in the years between? The truest, healthiest incentive to learn lies within us and is spontaneous. Wrong ideas about what and how children should learn made schoolmasters in the dark ages of education resort to the crude incentives of force. Less brutal but still damaging are many incentives practised today: rewards for the minority which are exclusive, carrying rejection for the unselected (e.g. prizes, prefect badges, comparative marks, ranking orders); and punishments which are no more than penalties, doing nothing to put the offender on a better path and help him to see the light.

Such incentives, whether rewards or punishments, act like purgatives on lazy bowels and are just as harmful. For as the bowel comes to expect stimulation from outside and will not work without it, so the child in this competition-ridden world behaves likewise.

The twin emotions of envy and jealousy, says Angus Wilson, are 'abnormally in evidence in our schooldays; it is then that the competitive spirit, fostered by the closed hot-house atmosphere, twists and twines its liana grip round the lives of the young – a bracing preparation, it is said, for the jungle world to come.'[1]

Fortunately a growing number of schools are beginning to reject these external spurs. But the path they wish to follow, as Michael Duane found at Risinghill, is not always an easy one. Had the lead not first been given by independent 'progressive' schools such as Summerhill and Dartington Hall today's achievements, such as they are, might not have been possible. Now, tentatively at first but with growing boldness, a handful of maintained schools are beginning to follow. But it is still very much a minority movement.

Houses, tutorial groups and social mixing

How useful are the house system and tutorial groups? The former exists in 92 per cent of the surveyed comprehensive schools, even (in attenuated form) in some of those whose basic organization is horizontal – i.e. lower, middle, and upper schools. Very occasionally the 'house' is an organization for games only. More frequently it extends to the social life of the school, and sometimes house groups are also classes for physical education, religious studies, crafts, and fine arts. Where house rooms or separate buildings are provided, the house is often an administrative centre too, with records, registers, reports, meals, cloakrooms, and many teams and clubs based on it.

There is no uniform pattern of house organization. A mixed school of 1,500 children may have five boys' houses and five girls' houses of 150 each, or it may have five mixed houses of 300 pupils each. It is difficult to see how the former arrangement, formally separating boys from girls in what is meant to be the kernel of a school's social life, can be justified in a comprehensive coeducational community.

1. *Sunday Times*, 10 December 1961.

Within the house there are sometimes tutorial groups, but the proportion (thirty-five per cent) is surprisingly low. Each member of staff is attached to a house, and nearly all assistant teachers, apart from the housemaster or housemistress, have a group of some thirty children each put in their care. It may be a group of either boys or girls, or of both boys and girls, all of one age; or it may be a cross-section of the school's age range, eleven to eighteen. In either case the tutor usually remains with his charges throughout their school life, though where personal antipathy exists between tutor and pupil, as must occasionally happen, the latter is transferred to another group.

There are obvious attractions in the idea of breaking the large school down into smaller divisions. The picture of a personal tutor watching over the interests of each child, in close touch with his parents, collecting and assimilating information about him from other members of staff, guiding his pupil in the choice of courses and the many personal problems of school life, is a fine, idealistic one. There is no doubt that not only in schools of over 1,000, but in most schools of 500 or so too, care of this kind is needed. It would transform the effectiveness of our education. All honour, then, to those heads who are trying to make the vision a reality.

We must, however, recognize that at present the reality often falls a good way short of the aim. Some teachers are good personal tutors of this kind, many are not. Even when everybody is pressed into service, the tutorial groups are too big. Frequent changes of staff, common in all types of school, wreck the idea of a longstanding relationship slowly built up. Further, the base from which the tutors start is an artificial and often inadequate one. Some of their flock they will teach rarely or never; and although this does not matter so much if they share out-of-class interests such as games or music or drama, it is difficult to manufacture points of contact where some common interest does not already exist. That is why the interests of pupils in a small school (say 300) are often better served by the whole body of staff, perhaps fifteen teachers in all, acting in concert. Among these fifteen there is a real chance that natural affinity and interests will exist between each pupil and at least one of the teachers – but in addition every pupil will know all the staff, and they will all feel both a corporate and a personal responsibility for each of the 300.

It may be felt that the staff of a house could fill this role; but this brings us to the artificial character and limited scope of any house system in a day school. The house is peripheral to the core of a school's activity, the main reason for a school's existence: work. The heart of the school is the classroom. It is through the difficulties and satisfactions of working together that the most genuine and lasting personal relations are built up, and the house in a day school simply has not got this basis. Relatively little teaching is done in the mixed-ability house groups.

The more one tries to overcome this weakness by stressing the importance of the house, the more one may be increasing the difficulties. Take, for example, a housemaster who does quite a lot of administration. He may, as one housemaster has observed, know the bright twenty per cent very well, the most troublesome twenty per cent even better, but the remaining sixty per cent very little. Moreover, the longer pupils stay at school and concentrate increasingly on the subjects they like, the more their real allegiance is given to the teachers of those subjects. Where – as is not uncommon – housemasters are non-graduates and perhaps never teach the fifth or sixth forms, they sometimes find the older members of their house growing away from them. Unless the housemaster can make the same subtle change of attitude towards a sixth-former which is taken for granted in grammar schools, he will find himself rapidly estranged and resented.

Segregation in separate houses, too, in many cases has little appeal for the sixth-former. He has little in common with the majority of pupils in the house; his horizon is widening, and he wants to revel in the society of his contemporaries. Most of them will be taking different courses, and he may see all too little of them if he stays largely confined to the house community.

If we are to have houses, there would seem to be a strong case for confining them to the eleven-to-sixteen age group, or even (bearing Wandsworth's lower school in mind) the thirteen-to-sixteen group, and bringing all the sixth-formers together, with their own large common-room and studies, at the top of the school. Apart from meeting their special needs, such a drawing together should have a unifying effect both symbolic and practical. Moreover it might then be possible to use only the really suitable members of staff as tutors. It would be interesting and informative if a school in Coventry, for example, with its strongly-developed house system, were to make special provision for the sixth form on these lines.

Wandsworth School in London – like Caludon Castle in Coventry – has a different combination of horizontal and vertical divisions: lower school eleven to thirteen (in the old grammar-school building but at the heart of the site) and houses thirteen to eighteen. By this means the gregarious younger boys get an ideal transition period between primary and full secondary education. They are not sealed off from the upper school, but are not thrown into it. There are informal contacts, and some teachers work in both lower and upper schools. Tutorial groups start at thirteen, and cover the adolescent stage when wise advice and sympathy from someone outside home are so often needed.

This pattern fits with that of the curriculum, with the foundation course to thirteen and biases developing beyond.

As Lenin and Stalin emphasized, theory without practice is sterile, practice without theory is blind. Principles must relate to empirical fact. For this reason my own preference, when faced with the need for smaller units within a large school, remains the horizontal division into lower and upper schools, with a move at fourteen.[1] An extra 'middle' division makes the whole thing too bitty, and moreover implies that basic general education, the 'foundation course', covers only two years instead of three. There is time enough to start specializing from fourteen onwards, particularly when the leaving age is raised to sixteen; and we must plan with that in mind.

Further, I believe that the natural choice as tutor for a group of day-school children is the form teacher, and that the form teacher should normally be the person who takes the class most often. Sometimes he may be able to move up the school with them a little way. Even during one year he is better placed than anyone else to fill the role of warden and guide described above. There are many teachers doing a competent job in these circumstances who find it impossible to forge a personal and group relationship out of little or nothing.

The boarding-school house is a substitute for the child's home. It is an acceptable substitute for a poor home, but a very moderate one for a good home. I am not yet convinced that its counterpart in a day school is necessary. Indeed, there are great dangers in schools attempting too much on their own. On the other hand, if the house system makes contact between school and home easier and more informal, and involves parents more closely in school affairs, it is well worth having. In one or two schools each

1. *Comprehensive Schools Today*, pp. 23-4.

house has its own parent-teacher association, which must assist this *rapport*.

In support of the house system is the conclusion drawn by A. G. Hind[1] that 'a different and "better" parent-teacher-pupil relationship can be developed through the house', and that 'children think about their houses, regard them with some affection/loyalty without loss of school pride.' Earlier, G. V. Pape[2] suggested that in a comprehensive school with a strongly-developed house system girls 'do not stick to their form-mates. They are just as likely to be found mixing with other members of their house who are in different forms.' On the other hand he found that in a grammar school without such a system they 'separate themselves off within the school, both inside the classroom and outside, into still finer ability groupings corresponding to the graded forms.'

Against this we must remember that Julienne Ford found streaming a much more potent factor than a house system in a comprehensive school; and the reservations of Margaret Miles should not be overlooked:

In the house system there is a tendency to encourage the sense of belonging by making each girl want to make her house the 'best' house . . . an idea which has always struck me as being immature and unfruitful of real educational and social development.[3]

I have suggested that work groups are the most natural, most cohesive social units. If this is so, it explains why English comprehensive schools are on the horns of a dilemma, and why some of them are so keen to devise an alternative and parallel social system (houses with tutorial groups) which will bring together pupils of all

1. *The comprehensive school with special reference to the house system*, Dip. Ed. thesis, University of Nottingham, 1964.

2. *Forum*, III, 2, pp. 71–4.

3. *op. cit.*, p. 31.

kinds of interest, background and ability. The practice of streaming children in groups of similar ability would otherwise mean that within one school there might develop cliques of clever children, gangs of backward ones. Certainly one might expect a tendency to drift apart, although this would be offset here and there by home friendships and special interests (e.g. games) which cut across the ability barrier.

The formation of very firm, exclusive circles based on common abilities and aptitudes is to some extent thwarted by the practice of 'setting', which means rearranging the children's classes according to their ability in different subjects. This in turn, however, involves a loss. There is such a thing as group personality, a highly important factor in any teaching situation; and it is difficult for such a personality to evolve if the stability of the group is constantly being upset by changes of membership. I recall the wise words of a former headmistress of Douglas Girls' High School : 'we try not to be too restless'.

Community Schools: some examples

An account of the remarkably rich, varied character and activities of anything like a representative sample of the established comprehensive schools would, like too much cream for tea, be liable to defeat one's object in providing it. Instead I shall attempt only a brief glimpse at what some of these schools are doing, in the hope that this will whet the appetite. There is much more to be found in the numerous monographs which are beginning to appear from particular schools.

The Lawrence Weston School in Bristol is a fine example of a large school on a city housing estate which is at the hub of local affairs. The school library is also a branch of the city library, and so a stock of more than 10,000 books, together with the services of a qualified librarian and two assistants, is available for the benefit of children and adults alike. Moreover it gives continuity, serving children throughout their lives at primary and secondary school, and after they have left. It is used, invaluably, at week-ends and during the holidays. Here is an arrangement which ought to be much more widespread – though it has indeed spread overseas, to both Jersey and the Isles of Scilly!

Lawrence Weston has an activities organizer, supernumerary to the school staff, who teaches part-time in school and does evening work. The responsibility which he takes enables the full-time teachers to contribute more freely and effectively out of school. Moreover parents and other adults lead such groups as the printing club, the pigeon club and the cycling proficiency class. Parents and older pupils have joined in the formation of a dance band; the school orchestra is often joined by members of staff, former pupils, and other local people; and the school regularly takes its music out to the parish church, the old people's home, and other schools.

The upper school is self-governing in its social affairs, and the Sixth Form Centre is open every week night for study and social activities. This open-minded attitude applies also, for example, to physical recreation, where alternatives to the traditional team games are provided in the form of such activities as judo, fencing, climbing, camping and field crafts, canoeing, trampolining, skating, cycling, badminton and tennis. On one afternoon a week young mothers join the sixth form in recreational and practical classes while their children are cared for in a pre-school play group within the school.

Lawrence Weston gives unusual emphasis to careers guidance, and in 1967 it joined with Marlborough College in starting a G CE 'A' level course in Business Studies.

The integration of school and neighbourhood is particularly advanced at Lawrence Weston School, but it is also

EVENING ACTIVITIES AT LOCKLEAZE SCHOOL, BRISTOL

	MONDAY	TUESDAY	WEDNESDAY	THURSDAY	FRIDAY
School Evening Activities	Archery 7.30	Drama 6.30	Badminton 6.30	Brass Band 7 p.m.	Latin 4 p.m.
	Gym & Trampoline 6.30	Train Your Dog 6.30	Come Caving 7 p.m.	Cookery for Boys 7 p.m.	
	Solve Your Problems 6.30 (Maths)	Chess 7 p.m.	Come & Experiment 6.30	Fishing 7 p.m.	
Begin 16 Sept.	Latin 4 p.m.	Light Craft 6.30	Typing Practice 7 p.m.	5-A-Side Football 7 p.m.	The Library
	Play Reading & Theatre Visits	Metalwork 6.30	Woodwork 6.30	Jewellery Making 6.30	will be
	Table Tennis 6.30	Music 'O' Level 4 p.m.		Light Craft 6.30	open each
	Typing for Beginners 7 p.m.	Needlework & Dressmaking 6.30		Music 'O' Level 4 p.m.	evening for
	Wheatsheaf Basketball 7.30	Swimming Training 7 p.m.		Physics for Fun 6.30	Homework
		Technical Drawing 6.30		Swimming (Learners) 6.30	
				Self Defence 6.30	
				Shorthand 7 p.m.	

Clubs	Boys' Brigade Swimming (Alt. Wks.) 7.30	Boys' Brigade Gym 7 p.m. 'Dings' Rugby Training 7 p.m.	Swimming 7 p.m. (Alt. Wks.) St James' Swimming 7.30 Comm. Ass. (Alt. Wks.)		A.T.C. 7 p.m. Boys' Brigade 7 p.m. Netball 7 p.m. St James' Gym (Girls) 7 p.m. Shaftesbury
Adult Education (15 yrs. upwards) Begins 30 Sept.	Pottery 7 p.m. Dressmaking 7 p.m. Woodwork 7 p.m.	Pottery 7 p.m. Painting 7 p.m. Cookery 7 p.m. Photography 7 p.m. Typing 7 p.m. Woodwork 7 p.m.	Football Training 7 p.m. St James' Football Training 7.30 p.m. Comm. Ass. Pottery 7 p.m.	Football Training 8 p.m. St James' Sculpture 7 p.m. Motor Engineering 7 p.m.	

a strong feature of the majority of the established comprehensives. An analysis of their local activities produces this remarkable list, some of them common to half of the schools in greater or lesser degree:

1. *Social service*, particularly to the old, the sick and the lonely, involving practical work in old people's homes and children's Homes. In one case social gatherings are arranged for a large immigrant community.

2. *Community studies* concerned with the environment, local development plans, and a school Civic Society. The interest sometimes reaches out to international affairs.

3. Earning and collecting money for *charities* such as Shelter, Oxfam, Save the Children Fund and local causes.

4. The multitude of activities in a *Community College or Centre*. At Stonehill High School in Leicestershire, for example, 1200–1500 parents use the buildings night and day, and almost every club and association in the area operates from Stonehill. The public use the swimming pool after 6 p.m.

5. *The Arts*, particularly music and drama. The local Eisteddfod is obviously important in Wales, for example at Llanfair Caereinion, where a quarter of the 300 pupils play musical instruments (strings, harp, brass and woodwind). But the arts flourish in the Black Country too. Northicote High School, Wolverhampton, which is linked with a Community Association, is unusually strong in music, with ballet, choir, and brass and string sections; and it produces its own record annually. In East Yorkshire, Hessle High School has a strong tradition of instrumental playing which covers all ability groups. It has a full school orchestra, string orchestra, string quartet, junior orchestra, folk group, and senior and junior brass bands. All these take part in local festivals, and the brass bands

have toured Belgium and Germany. In addition there are a dance band, jazz band and choirs. Many more examples of the work of schools in this field could be given.

6. *Evening Institute* classes are commonly housed in the school and staffed by teachers.

7. *Work experience* for children, usually in the fourth or fifth year, with local firms. Four-fifths of the fifth form boys and girls at Longslade School, Birstall, in Leicestershire, have voluntarily spent from two days to two weeks in this way.

8. *Joint teams*, e.g. in football, cricket, basketball, for school pupils and local youth.

9. *A termly meeting* (at Hessle) of housemasters and other interested teachers with doctors, ministers, police, probation officers, child and education welfare officers.

10. *Subject 'teach-ins'* by staff for parents.

11. *Life-saving and shore rescue.*

12. In the countryside, *Young Farmer's Clubs* and the sensible, practical arrangements which appeal there : 'Farmers take our sheep, we take their cows for exchange of eatage' (Settle High School).

Although links with the neighbourhood are becoming strong, this does not mean that the schools are at all parochial. On the contrary, school journeys to Scandinavia and to East, Central and Western Europe are a regular feature of life in many schools, and a few go still further afield : for example pupils of Brookfield School, Kirkby, have been on educational cruises to Russia, the Mediterranean and North Africa. Adventure courses, including climbing and canoeing, are fairly common, and several schools have the use of a clubhouse of some kind (perhaps a converted barn or abandoned railway station) in the hills.

Everywhere there is a dual concern: that all children, regardless of ability or home background, should have maximum opportunity for self-fulfilment; and along with this a concern for excellence. The latter often comes out in the high standard of group performances, such as orchestral music, but it is seen also with individuals: for example the broadcast of a poem by a fourteen-year-old boy from Mountgrace High School, Hinckley.

A review of the magnificent achievements of so many comprehensive schools, quite outside their classroom obligations, must fill the unprejudiced observer with respect. He will ask, 'What motivates these teachers to give themselves so wholeheartedly?'

The answer must be that they are inspired by a faith, and by the desire to show that that faith is well-based. 'This', says one headmaster, 'is essentially a place of individual values. Courses are arranged for individuals, not individuals fitted to courses. ... We stress the danger of generalization about groups of human beings: therefore we refuse to label our own pupils and seek to develop the particular talents and to stimulate the particular contribution of each person.'

Many are now thinking and speaking the same language. 'We believe', says another head, 'above all in a caring community: good personal relations and the constant encouragement of pupils at all stages, with a wide range of subjects and activities to give everybody the best possible chance of finding his or her proper place and making the fullest use of natural endowment.'

The way ahead

The established comprehensive school, then, is very much a school for the community. But with widespread reorganization the picture in the years ahead is bound to be very uneven.

Many schools are still withdrawn, after the rather stilted, aloof English custom. Too many teachers still tend to think of the school as a tight professional preserve which is their concern and nobody else's. They even manage to sell this to parents. Parents' Associations, like football supporters' clubs, often accept as their aim 'assistance without interference'.

There is always a borderland where the special interests and qualifications of parent and teacher overlap. Should school uniform be compulsory or even 'expected'? What restrictions on children's dress, hair style, adornments, are reasonable? Who is the final authority on conduct out of school? Should corporal punishment be used, and if so, in what circumstances? Ought a headmaster to have the power to forbid a seventeen-year-old cricketer to play for a league side on Saturday afternoon, and to compel him instead to turn out for the school in a game much inferior in standard?

Where teachers and parents, with conviction, hold opposing views on such matters, clashes are bound to arise. In England we and the courts back the teachers almost automatically. A teacher has to do something manifestly wrong before he is condemned. We *want* him to be thought right. Teachers too easily forget this when they complain of 'inferior status'. To what other classes of the community does this spontaneous support apply? By contrast, a solicitor or an accountant is given much less mercy if his conduct is brought into question. Can it be that teachers as a body have an uneasy conscience because they do not and of course cannot live up to the high standards which their former pupils want them to have?

The idol always has feet of clay. Goldsmith's village schoolmaster was, doubtless, something of an impostor:

> And still they gazed, and still the wonder grew
> That one small head could carry all he knew.

Children invest parents and teachers with godlike qualities. With maturity comes disillusion. The great test of adults is how far they can change worship into understanding love rather than hurt disappointment. For this reason it is dangerous, and a sign of inner weakness, for adults to seek to maintain their prestige by extending the authoritarian role unchanged from infants to adolescents. The adolescents of today are the parents of tomorrow.

In North America the parent has much more say, both in the social education of the child and in his choice of curriculum. 'When the chips are down,' a Canadian headmaster tells me, 'it's the parent and pupil who decide.'

Here, in the relations between school and local society, is a wonderful opportunity for adult education. Parents and teachers have one binding interest, the child's welfare. Because most adults become parents at some time or other, they are nearly all approachable through a medium which concerns them intimately. I wish that the Workers' Educational Association, instead of providing quite so many classes in philosophy, psychology, art, and music, and becoming a purveyor of middle-class 'culture' to would-be intellectuals, could take a leading role in this field. It is possibly the only way of involving the working class *as a whole* in the sort of education which they find meaningful. Through the intimate interweaving of school and local society, the promotion of a classless, communal culture is a practical possibility: not, I repeat, a flat, common culture, but one whose basic values (such as truth, tolerance, courage, justice, and beauty) would be accepted by all, one leading to lives rich in purpose and variety.

But the WEA cannot act alone. The churches, too, like other voluntary bodies, should be involved. Above all, the teachers' associations must throw aside the shield of reserve behind which they shelter from the honest scrutiny of their fellows. They must stop sitting on the fence on matters of clear principle because they fear for the vested interests of their members. If they are to earn the regard of the community, as they certainly yearn for it, they should today be actively promoting the most lively and searching discussion around their schools concerning what goes on inside them.

The first English comprehensive schools were, on the whole, too self-contained. They should not be blamed for this. Here, as in so much else, they inherited a long tradition. Moreover they were so preoccupied with winning acceptance on current standards – examination results, conduct, cultural activities, and so on – that they had little time, even when the inclination was there, to venture beyond the frontier of contemporary educational practice. Sometimes local political circumstances were such that it would have been foolish to do so. The art of timing is at the heart of success in men's affairs, and the climate has not always favoured bold enterprises.

But that climate has now changed in startling fashion, and we must take the current when it serves. In human life we cannot mark time for long. If we do not go forward, we slip back. When we cease to grow, we start to die. The time is ripe for a major advance in the relations between our community schools and the community itself.

Seven years ago I found that only forty-eight out of a hundred schools had a parent-teacher association or similar body. Today's proportion is still only fifty-one per cent. It is felt by many heads of schools without such associations that they are liable to be dominated by middle-class parents: 'The parents I want to see are those who would never come – parents of the C stream.' They prefer meetings specially and separately arranged for parents of particular classes, first year, second year, and so on.

But although there is much to be said for such special meetings, it is not usually possible for parents at such gatherings to do more than discuss their own children's progress with the teachers. There is little or no opportunity to discover and discuss common ground with other parents – and one has an uncomfortable feeling that many heads do not want this. Nor is the absence of C-stream parents from parent-teacher associations a good reason for depriving other parents of the chance to discuss educational principles as applied in their children's school. It may be a reason for questioning the existence of categories like 'C stream' at all. It may indicate the need for teachers to go out and get to know absentee parents in their own homes and bring them in – but not to close down channels of contact for everyone.

The difficulty of parents getting to and from school in the evenings is a big obstacle in rural areas. But, as we have seen, that very difficulty inspired Henry Morris to set up his village colleges in Cambridgeshire. The village college idea is a two-way current. People pour in to the centre, teachers go out to the villages and hamlets. The outgoing is essential. There is room for much further development in this aspect of the work of comprehensive schools as a whole, even though in eighty-seven per cent of the established comprehensives the buildings are used by people of the neighbourhood at evenings or weekends for social and/or educational activities.

The big deficiency, which is not peculiar to comprehensive schools, is the lack of direct contact by teachers with their pupils' homes. American schools have their guidance departments of specially qualified people. We need them too; but it is essential that when they come they shall aid teachers to do a bigger and wider job, including welfare, not allow them to withdraw still more into specialist teaching alone.

The most valuable contacts are often those made informally by people sharing in local activities. It happens easily enough in country towns; it is beginning to happen, as we have seen, in the cities and housing estates where it is still more valuable. But ideally this demands that teachers shall live in the district served by the school – as a few are starting to do at Kirkby – and a great many prefer to 'get away from it all' by living elsewhere. One sympathizes, for they are often tired from overwork. But could the boarding school survive if its staff went as far away as possible as soon as formal schooling ended? Could the priest feel that he earned even his meagre salary if he merely conducted the services, the church council and vestry meetings, and the Sunday School outing?

I have criticized much in English schools and teachers. But they have their strengths as well as their weaknesses, and the former must not be swept away with the latter. One of their most valuable features in the past has been the pastoral care bestowed on their pupils. Bigger schools, a shortage of teachers, improved transport, the greater mobility of society, segregation at eleven – all these have gone far to destroy it. Perhaps this is the most important reason why boarding schools are popular; they are the best substitute we have for the real thing. But the genuine, established comprehensive schools are now making an ideal into reality. With the proof of their achievements now with us there can be no doubt that it is in the neighbourhood school, in which children, parents, teachers and others meet and mingle, that the fullest preparation for a rich, purposeful life in a democratic society can be gained.

4. Marlborough College and Risinghill

IN my first chapter I likened our divided system of secondary education to a three-lane track. The 'public' schools are on the favoured inside lane, but this privileged position arouses far less public passion and even interest than the division between the middle (grammar) and outside ('modern') lanes, because the so-called 'public' schools are remote from the lives of the real public, and assumed to be quite out of reach of the latter's children. This situation always reminds me of Lazaraus and the rich man :

Between us and you there is a great gulf fixed, so that they which would pass from hence to you cannot; neither can they pass to us that would come from thence.

Two events in the 1960s brought home just how deep and wide, and at present unbridgeable, is the gulf in England between the schools for the rich and the schools for the poor. They also raised sharply the most profound issues which result from acceptance of the comprehensive principle.

Risinghill

In 1960 the London County Council opened a new comprehensive school in the borough of Islington – a few minutes' walk from King's Cross and even nearer to Pentonville Jail. It was a sordid, depressed neighbourhood. Many of the houses were rotten with damp and decay, and they left their mark on the unfortunate families who had no choice but to inhabit them. It was an area of violence and prostitution, in which many children did not know which of the men who in turn shared their mother's bed was their father.

Children grew up to take violence for granted. Whenever their mother was tired or unable to cope, she would slap them automatically. Survival in the jungle of the streets meant joining a gang, and proving that you were as hard and aggressive as the next boy or girl. Some primary school teachers, living outside the area and seeing many of their charges as little toughs who had to be tamed, felt that corporal punishment was a necessary weapon in their struggle to maintain order. There were no fewer than nineteen different nationalities, and a quarter of the people were not English. Over all loomed the shadow of Pentonville: what hope, what faith could a frightened, beaten child have for the future when he knew that across the road a man was being hanged, a periodical reminder of the hatred in the hearts of adults?

The new school was certainly a neighbourhood school – but a 'neighbourhood' of the depressed classes only, with social problems greater even than those of Kirkby. It was not comprehensive in the London sense of having a balanced intake of ability; when it opened in 1960 it had only one per cent of the children in the top grade of ability, some 50 per cent in the bottom grade. If ever a school cried out for maximum aid in the form of a generous supply of first-class teachers, well-planned buildings and good equipment, with sympathetic support from the local education authority, that school was Risinghill. It served what was an obvious 'educational priority area' long before the Plowden Committee coined that ugly, deadening phrase.

The man appointed to the key job of headmaster was Michael Duane, a left-wing ex-Army major who had previously been head of two 'modern' schools in Hertfordshire and Suffolk and had clashed with conservative elements at both places in the process of building up his schools on progressive lines. Duane was a friend of A. S. Neill, whose permissive ideas and practice have had a world-wide impact. But Neill enjoyed the freedom (except for financial worries) afforded by an independent school. Was it possible successfully to transplant the Neill approach to a school provided and controlled by a local authority, even one with the high educational reputation of the London County Council?

Certainly Alex Bloom, with much the same outlook, had achieved a great deal at Saint George-in-the-East, a 'modern' school in Cable Street, Stepney. But Bloom was regarded rather as a curiosity, and his school was, after all, 'only' a secondary modern. Odd behaviour and strange experiments with children already written off as failures were one thing; but at Risinghill the comprehensive image (and with it the reputation of the London County Council) was itself on trial. Experiment was bound to be watched more apprehensively; certainly there was less room for failure.

Duane, impressive in both appearance and personality, seemed well fitted to make the attempt. He had the right kind of down-to-earth experience. He was a fluent speaker, a hard worker, a man easily approached by children and parents; social outcasts sensed his sympathy and his readiness to give himself unstintingly to help them.

These were fine qualities and rare qualities: headmasters of this calibre are men to be prized and supported. But no headmaster is perfect, and one criticism subsequently levelled against Michael Duane – justly or not – was that he expected his assistant teachers to be more mature than in fact they were, indeed than most of us are. Some felt that he expected them to labour in this very exacting vineyard as wholeheartedly as he did himself, without requiring words of appreciation or encouragement from him, without even the direction they expected from him: 'we have the right to be led', they said. In short,

while he practised leadership by example they expected,
and were disappointed at not receiving, leadership of a more
traditional kind. So they began to feel insecure, and mis-
understanding grew up between Duane and some (though
not all) of the staff.

When such a situation develops, who is right and who
is wrong is not the real problem – it is the existence of the
situation itself. In such circumstances the tension is often
relieved by help and sympathey from officials inside and outside the school. Unfortunately it seems that Duane had
little such advantage. He stood alone, the central figure in
what was indeed a great dramatic tragedy such as the world
of education makes it its business to study but rarely itself
provides. But I am anticipating.

Despite Michael Duane's radical outlook Risinghill
opened on quite orthodox, even conservative, lines. There
was good reason for this. Although the buildings were
new, the school was largely an amalgam of no fewer than
four local single-sex secondary 'modern' or technical
schools. Some teachers whose outlook was conservative,
and perhaps embittered by the depressing conditions in
which they had served for too long, were brought unwill-
ingly into a situation which cried out for men and women,
preferably with some experience, but above all who were
young in heart and eager to accept as daunting a challenge
as one could find anywhere in England. Many older children, too, resented the move, and fights between gangs from
the different schools inevitably heralded the birth of
Risinghill.

So Duane began cautiously – and in fact the school's
organization continued on traditional lines thereafter.

The children were grouped in streams broadly according
to ability. There were prefects, prizes and speech days.
There was a house system of the kind common in other

schools. There was even corporal punishment. Much as Duane himself disliked caning, the ban on it did not originally come from him: it resulted from a staff decision to discontinue caning, which was taken at a meeting at which Duane was not present. What Duane did do, to the teachers' surprise and dismay, was to inform the school of the decision. They thought this was inviting trouble. He, on the other hand, had assumed that the children obviously needed to know, as a matter of course: otherwise they would be subject to a threat which had no foundation and would be a living lie.

What happened thereafter has been told in great detail by Leila Berg in what will rank in future as one of the most unusual yet significant contributions ever made to English educational history.[1] Her book is both passionate and partisan, but it is also a meticulously-compiled record of her very thorough investigation of the whole affair. Add to this that she is a writer with the ability to capture atmosphere and portray character, and a sense of the tragic inevitability of the drama which she chronicles, and one begins to appreciate how different in quality is this piece of work from the turgid prose which we professional educators usually inflict upon our fellows.

During the first three years of its short life Risinghill had its successes in spite of the constant difficulties. In 1960 five pupils had passed in some subjects at GCE 'O' level. In 1964 forty-two passed in one to six subjects at 'O' level, and two pupils (an English boy and a Turkish-Cypriot boy) went to universities. When the school opened in 1960 there were ninety-eight children on probation; in 1964 there were nine.

Among the memorable events was a moving nativity play, of which the *Islington Gazette* wrote:

1. *Risinghill: Death of a Comprehensive School* (Penguin, 1968).

Not for Risinghill the worn-out gimmicks.... For Risinghill – the impact of luxurious costumes just like King Herod and the three kings from the East must have worn. For Risinghill – the impact of a thunderingly majestic orchestra which accompanied a grandiose choir. For Risinghill – the impact of a multiracial cast adding oriental splendour and striking authenticity to this most exciting of tales. As I left Risinghill Street and walked in the chilly December night air down Chapel Market, I wept slowly with emotion at the greatest nativity play I have ever had the honour and privilege to see.

And (as Leila Berg adds) for Risinghill, too, a real baby.

By 1964 the school had a West Indian head boy and a Greek-Cypriot head girl; and at a time when Greeks and Turks were slaughtering each other in Cyprus children of these nationalities were living happily together at Risinghill. Early in 1965 the Cultural Attaché of the Cyprus High Commission protested against the proposed closure of the school and said: 'Risinghill has succeeded in doing something the United Nations cannot do.'

Inside the school I myself recall particularly the creative work being done in art, and the complete absorption of a 'King of the Teds' in his work there. I remember, too, that natural, friendly, secure way in which children came to Duane's study, as they did with Bloom in Stepney, and as they might to a loved father: they took it for granted that they were welcome. 'Suffer the little children to come unto me, and forbid them not' is an injunction which too many head teachers, weighed down by administrative chores as they are, have forgotten.

It was all in vain. In a school beset by constant problems resulting from shortage of teachers (particularly suitable teachers), an ill-planned collection of buildings, and the personal difficulties which many children inevitably brought with them from home, Michael Duane found himself at loggerheads with a substantial section of the staff.

They demanded the security of the orthodox methods, particularly for the enforcement of order and acceptable behaviour, with which they were familiar. Duane, unable to betray either his own conscience or the children who had come to trust him, found it impossible to concede such demands. His local inspector was unsympathetic, the local education authority seemingly worried about the rumours that were being spread and the bad reputation for both comprehensive schools and the London County Council which might result.

At this point the only way of saving the situation was decisive action by the local education authority. What was needed – what, indeed, Michael Duane surely had every reason to expect from the opening of the school – was, first, continued public demonstration that what Duane was attempting had the Authority's backing; secondly, deliberate attraction of capable, interested teachers to fill vacancies as they occurred (not impossible once teachers know that the Authority is firmly backing the experiment); and thirdly, steady reassurance and support for the head in the difficulties which were bound to occur.

I believe that such a policy would not only have saved Risinghill, and kept faith with the parents and children who had hoped for so much from the provision of a new comprehensive school; it would have greatly enhanced the reputation of the London County Council itself. For Risinghill was a test case: if a comprehensive school could succeed there, it could succeed anywhere.

Alas, it appears that the LCC's outlook was far too staid, conservative and timid to permit such an approach. Perhaps Duane made tactical mistakes: what pioneer does not? But his objectives were unquestionably right, and his personal contribution in many ways magnificent. He needed help, not opposition, and his great gifts were a godsend to any Authority which really believed in what he was trying to do. Amid the maelstrom of conflicting accounts and opinions one can only record one's personal conclusions. My own feeling, then as now, was one of immense sadness. There were no villains; in such crises 'passions spin the plot'. So a potential triumph was turned by little men into a disaster. The LCC giant lacked the vision to match its physical stature. On what (despite denials) was widely accepted as the pretext of falling numbers, and in spite of urgent protests from many parents, in 1965 Risinghill School was closed.

Somehow it was appropriate that at the polls a mere three years later the long-standing local champions of a democratic Labour movement, and the self-proclaimed leaders of progressive education, should follow Michael Duane into the wilderness.

The tragedy of Risinghill was a tragedy not only for its headmaster and its children, and for the Inner London Education Authority (successor to the LCC). It was a tragedy for England. London's action was a signal to other authorities to mark time, to postpone a deep-searching attack on the social and education problems of the depressed areas. Such an attack is not achieved by mere reorganization; a comprehensive school can be as authoritarian as any grammar or 'modern' school – indeed, because people expect better things of it an authoritarian comprehensive school may cause positive disillusionment with reform.

And yet it was not an unrelieved tragedy. Because Risinghill became a *cause célèbre*, the issues at stake came to be more widely discussed than would otherwise have been likely. Student teachers, for example, cannot avoid facing these issues – and whatever their conclusions, they know that the attitudes and practices they will adopt in school are vitally important to our society. The theoretical case for linking home and school, for revising our ideas on the role and authority of the teacher, for putting the old incentives into the melting pot, takes on a new and real significance in the context of Risinghill.

Martyrdom, indeed, is sometimes the best guarantee of survival in the minds of men.

In the same year that Risinghill was closed an experiment of a very different nature was begun.

The 'public' schools

Although the future of the 'public' schools had not yet aroused strong feelings within the nation, many heads of these schools had watched the growth of comprehensive education in the State system with interest and sometimes with concern. Mr Crosland was now about to set up the Public Schools Commission 'to advise on the best way of integrating the public schools with the State system of education'. The time for reappraisal had clearly arrived.

When the man in the street hears or reads of the 'public' schools he thinks, perhaps, of a few famous names: Eton, Harrow, Winchester; a personality like Arnold of Rugby; or the story of 'Tom Brown's Schooldays'. He may recall half-forgotten notions about fagging, dormitory rags, and the religion of games – its litany being concerned with a bumping pitch and a blinding light, and the eleventh commandment: 'Play up, play up, and play the game'. It is a vague and confused picture, but also a romantic one, if only because boys' school stories have so largely centred on boarding school life.

The one definite thing about the 'public' schools is that they are not public. There is no standard definition and many day schools and minor boarding schools, whether independent or aided by the Department of Education and Science and local authorities, lay claim to the label of 'public' school. But the schools which people have in mind, however vaguely when they use the term, are in fact the bigger, independent boys' boarding schools, about eighty in number, which are represented on the Headmasters' Conference. These can be subdivided roughly into three categories: (a) the large and famous schools of ancient foundation, such as Winchester, Eton and Westminster; (b) the grammar schools which in the eighteenth and early nineteenth centuries expanded and came to cater for much more than local needs, including Harrow, Rugby, Shrewsbury, Repton and Uppingham; (c) the schools which were founded in the middle of the nineteenth century to provide for the sons of rich industrialists the same kind of gentlemen's education as the sons of the landed gentry enjoyed (or perhaps I should say 'endured') at the existing 'public' schools. These new foundations included Marlborough (founded in 1843), Bradfield (1850), Wellington (1852) and Clifton (1862).

The first two groups of schools have provided much material for the biographer, for the reputation of each school was decided almost entirely by the calibre of its headmaster. Samuel Butler, who was appointed to Shrewsbury in 1798, made scholarship the first objective in the school, just as Thomas Arnold, who came to Rugby in 1828, emphasized moral tone and the responsibility of senior boys. Later Thring at Uppingham was to insist on the right of every boy to some privacy in a study of his own, and to stress the importance of music and art in education. Sanderson followed up Thring's ideas at Oundle from 1892 to 1922, and made sweeping reforms in the curriculum, such as the introduction of large workshops and the modern approach to science. Not all heads were great men however. Under Dr Keate, headmaster of Eton from 1809 to 1834, nearly two hundred senior boys were taken in a single class; and this irascible disciplinarian once flogged his confirmation class under the belief that they were defaulters sent along for punishment.

Ragging and bullying were quite common features of 'public' school life. The new schools, which had no harmful traditions, nevertheless copied the older schools and could offer scenes which were just as bad. In 1929 Sir Cyril Norwood wrote:

Let us for a moment consider Marlborough, filled with boys in 1843, largely from country rectories. By 1850 this had become a school which took a new boy, a child of eight years of age, tied him to a bench in Upper School, where there were throngs of boys present, and branded him with an anchor on the forearm by means of a red hot poker. Seventy-one years later I saw the scar, a mark extending from the forearm to the wrist. There was, so far as the victim was aware, no punishment, though he had to spend three weeks in the Sick House.[1]

As the years passed the 'public' schools changed little. In 1917 Alec Waugh published *The Loom of Youth* which had largely been written while the author was still at school. This classic tale was a fierce indictment of boarding school life at that time.

Interest in the 'public' schools was revived in the early 1940s. One by-product of the war of 1939–45 was a great surge of interest in education and particularly in the provision for all of equal opportunity in education. This led to a series of attacks on the 'public' schools as the home of privilege, places where the sons of rich parents had an education superior to anything that local schools could provide. Many wanted to bring the 'public' schools more closely into touch with the national educational system, so that their superior qualities might be made available to children of parents who could not afford to pay the fees.

It was this demand which led to the appointment of the

1. *The English Tradition in Education* (1929), quoted in Lamb, *The English at School* (Allen & Unwin), p. 170.

Fleming Committee which in 1944 issued its report on the 'public' schools and their relation to the general educational system. This, in brief, recommended that the 'public' schools should set aside twenty-five per cent of their entrance places each year for boys who had been educated at primary schools in the national system. They would be selected by regional interviewing boards and granted bursaries by the Board of Education, as it then was, to cover their fees and maintenance. The Fleming recommendations were never officially adopted, although the local education authorities have been encouraged to make their own arrangements with nearby 'public' schools. Under the 1944 Act local education authorities are required to

have regard to the expediency of securing the provision of boarding accommodation either in boarding schools or otherwise for pupils for whom education as boarders is considered by their parents and by the authority to be desirable.

However although a few local authorities have made such arrangements with 'public' schools in or near their area, most authorities have taken no action. Their reasons may be summarized as follows:

First, expense. Fees at such boarding schools now range from £350 to more than £600 a year.

Secondly, local grammar schools do not want to be deprived of the best boys of their district.

Thirdly, political opponents argue that to bolster up the 'public' schools by letting them flourish on the best material from the maintained schools would be like giving a blood transfusion to a parasite; it would perpetuate class distinction, not remove it.

Fourthly, some opponents feel that the education at a 'public' school is essentially bad. There are some saving qualities, it is true: spacious grounds, excellent equipment and teaching, and opportunity for cultural pursuits. But there is no reason why a good day school should not provide all these, while on the other side must be set many features which are anathema to 'progressive' educators, such as the rule of senior boys over the juniors, often associated with the power of beating; the incentives of competition and punishment which the average 'public' school man still thinks are the only effective ones, not only in school, but in society at large; and the one sex, monastic community with its unnatural views and experience of sex and often the unhappy emotional consequences for boys in adult life.

Even Alec Waugh, for all his criticisms of detail, could not see that it was the nature of the system which produced the things that horrified him. These words of his were written in 1922, but 'public' school men will be saying just the same things in 1972:

Any critic of the public schools is immediately driven into a false position. If anyone breathes a word against them now, he is labelled a revolutionary. It is assumed that politically he is a socialist, that he wishes to substitute cooperation for competition, that he is a harbinger of red ruin. Nothing as a matter of fact is further from the truth. The majority of assailants are anything but socialists. They consider an enlightened oligarchy the ideal form of government. No one wants to destroy the public schools. No one would be so foolish.

And again:

It is a regrettable fact, but a true one, that human beings will only work under the influence of a bribe or of a threat.

More recently, further self-criticism has come from within the 'public' schools. Perhaps the most penetrating study is that by two Wykehamists, Bishop and Wilkinson.[1] They point to such factors as 'the accent barrier' to social mobility, and the pull in competition for top jobs. It may

1. *Winchester and the Public School Elite* (Faber & Faber, 1967).

not be surprising to learn that the Conservative Prime Minister, Stanley Baldwin, told the Harrow Association in 1923, 'I remember how in previous governments there had been four, perhaps five Harrovians, and I determined to have six'. It is more significant that a generation later a Labour Prime Minister, Clement Attlee, could be similarly influenced: 'Other things being equal I didn't see why I should not select someone from my own school [Haileybury] . . . I chose Geoffrey Freitas.'

In one notable description of Winchester Bishop and Wilkinson picture a world utterly remote from the abysmally mean existence of the people of Risinghill:

To the thoughtful outsider it must be amazing that such a wealth of land and stone should house a mere five hundred boys. Playing field upon playing field; a soaring chapel; . . . a myriad of walls, gates, walks and archways, each a historic name to be dutifully learned by the newcomer. A place of beauty and bewitching atmosphere, but a beauty and atmosphere that is essentially medieval, binding frail man within a great feudal community.

For all its beauty, Bishop and Wilkinson are critical of the appropriateness of this monastic environment as a preparation for the good life, for the development of emotionally mature and happy adults. 'Historically, the primary aim of the private schools has *not* been to produce husbands and fathers; it has been to supply government, the professions and, more recently, business, with leaders.'

Here, perhaps, is the nub of our increasing uneasiness about the 'public' schools. A society which is led by men dedicated to their careers, by and large at the expense of emotional balance and stable personal relationships – or, in A. S. Neill's neat phrase, who put head before heart – will inevitably reflect these false values. But such is the awesome reputation of the 'public' schools in England that very few dare ask themselves (much less voice openly) what is really the basic question: 'Are these really good schools? Would their principles and practice be found acceptable if they were to be brought into the State system and set alongside the local schools, whose virtues are unsung?'

The Marlborough experiment

In 1961 Marlborough College acquired a new headmaster, John Dancy. Dancy had been a pupil and master at Winchester and later head of Lancing. He was more acutely aware of the changing social scene than some of his contemporaries, and had a reputation for moderately liberal views. When a survey by Michael Young and Peter Wilmott in the Swindon area indicated that one-third of parents with sons aged fifteen might favour their boarding at a school like Marlborough, and that four-fifths of these would be willing to make some contribution towards the fees, Dancy welcomed the possibility of an experiment in integration. Money was provided by Swindon and the Department of Education and Science, and from other sources. In September 1965 twenty-one boys who had previously taken 'O' levels at local schools in Swindon and Wiltshire entered the College, joining there another 800 boys – Marlborough College boys who had, of course, been recruited in the traditional way.

From the outset the experiment was covered by a research unit. The head of the unit, Dr Royston Lambert, and one of his assistants, Susan Stagg, have described the aims, progress and outcome of the experiment in a paper which is a model of objective yet incisive reporting.[1]

Eleven of 'the Swindon boys', as the new group came to be called, were from grammar schools in Swindon, and

1. Paper Three, 'Integration: a Pilot Scheme', in *New Wine in Old Bottles?* (Occasional Papers on Social Administration no. 28, Bell, 1968).

ten from 'modern' schools in Swindon, Chippenham and Malmesbury. All, however, had gained at least four 'O' levels and all were about sixteen years of age.

The omens for successful integration were reasonably good – certainly much better than would be the case if such transfer were forced on unwilling schools or pupils. It turned out that the Young–Wilmott estimates had been over-optimistic : when it came to the point most local boys would not hear of going to the College, whatever their parents thought. But the chosen twenty-one had less strong local ties than most; they were moreover ambitious to get on in the world, and convinced that the teaching and academic standards at the College would be far better than those of their local schools. Theoretically they knew that conditions would be different in many ways, but they were prepared to adjust. They wanted the experiment to succeed – indeed for them, entrusting two critically important years of their lives to it, it was vital that it should succeed.

At the College, too, much care had been taken to prepare the ground. Staff and boys knew what was afoot, and had been encouraged to be understanding and helpful. The Swindon boys were divided among five houses whose housemasters were keen on the scheme. Certain rules were relaxed for their benefit – for example, they were allowed to go home on Saturday and Sunday afternoons (but not to stay there overnight).

Nevertheless, despite these auspicious factors (say Miss Stagg and Dr Lambert)

By the end of the two years three boys had been a focus of continuous behaviour problems, one of the most favourably disposed housemasters declared that he would not volunteer to have boys on integration schemes in his house again without more safeguards, three of the boys suffered periodically from what the school doctor diagnosed as 'stress symptoms', and the majority, though well-adjusted, contributive and satisfied, had challenged some of the fundamental values of the public school embodied in its structure.

What went wrong?

In a sense, nothing went wrong. What happened was a clash of two different cultures, each of which had only dimly been understood by those who belonged to the other. The lesson is that goodwill alone is not enough: reformers also need understanding, understanding moreover which is born of personal experience. The masters and boys of Marlborough belonged to a world apart from that of the Swindon boys. Their unconscious attitudes are revealed most clearly in little ways such as the use by some Marlburians of the terms 'yokels' and 'proles' for local people. Most public school masters have never been in any but a public school as pupil or teacher, most housemasters have never even taught outside their present school.

The Swindon boys were rudely awakened from any illusion they may have had about comfort and amenities at the College. At first only two of these 16-year-old boys even shared a study with someone else; the others endured, and had to try to work, in the Spartan conditions of a large classroom. It is extremely difficult for anyone who has known the ease and comfort of working at home to adapt to such a life. The interruptions of other boys, the frequent bells, the rules about bedtime and lights out, are maddening restrictions on one's freedom and make application to one's studies extremely difficult.

Restrictions on social life were also irksome – on the use of a motor bike (in an area where public transport is poor), on meetings with girl friends, on the simple stroll into town when one felt like a change of surroundings. The Swindon boys felt that the school looked down on football: 'They've got thirty rugby pitches and one for football . . . they think it's not gentlemanly.' How many 'public' school people begin to understand how central to the lives of millions of people in England is the Saturday afternoon football ritual?

Then there was the denial of a status which the Swindon boys had taken for granted. Had they stayed at their local schools they would have been first-year sixth-formers, important people with a considerable amount of freedom. At Marlborough they were not rated as sixth-formers at all in their first year; indeed, we are told that only three of the twenty-one ever attained sixth-form status. They found themselves under the jurisdiction of boys of the same age or even younger. Further, much that the Marlburians took seriously – 'working for House', or 'shouting for House' – seemed childish.[1]

The situation was aggravated by another clash of totally different attitudes, this time on the nature of authority in school. In most State schools nowadays 'prefects' mainly perform minor administrative jobs, helping out the staff; they rarely attempt to impose their own authority on their fellows. At Marlborough house captains seemed to rank in importance equally with the housemaster himself and exercised enormous power, including the power of beating. They took their responsibilities with a seriousness that to the Swindon boys seemed ludicrous. A quotation by Lambert from elsewhere nevertheless seems applicable here:

I wasn't happy [said one] with the way people's souls were pulled to pieces by 17–18-year-old prefects who seemed to have only a very limited experience of humanity on which to draw in judging others.[2]

A few of the Swindon boys could not accept an authority which seemed to them wholly unreasonable. They

1. *cf.* the comment by Margaret Miles, p. 139 above.
2. *op. cit.*, Paper One, p. 41.

defied it repeatedly, with a bluntness which only served to alienate the Marlburians still more. A handful ignored the rules and lied persistently under investigation. One seventeen-year-old boy was eventually beaten.

There were other distasteful features such as compulsory religion and compulsory games (even those who were keen on games found the time and importance given to them excessive). What seemed a certain snobbery grated: for example the wearing of dinner jackets at ritual dinners, and the attitude to servants. When a Swindon boy politely addressed an adult college servant as 'sir' he was corrected by a Marlburian. And (in the words of the research team) 'most found that the homosexual talk and underlife of the school were repugnant'. Marlborough, it will be recalled, was established primarily for the sons of clergymen.

All this might just possibly have been worthwhile had the Swindon boys' academic expectations been fulfilled. But here again there was disappointment. They had not realized that, with practically all boys staying to 18, 'A' level classes were as large as, or larger than, those in grammar schools; and doubtless the other frustrations which they were experiencing hindered concentration. The wide range of extra-curricular activities which was available, such as music and painting, and in which they gradually began to take more part, may also have been a distraction.

Whatever the reasons, 'A' level results of the Swindon boys, though not disastrous, were disappointing. They fell below those of a comparable group of Marlburians in both quantity and quality. It seems likely that they would have done at least as well had they stayed in a local grammar school, and would have had a happier time into the bargain.

This brief summary cannot do justice to a brilliant paper which ought to be read by all teachers and educational administrators, and by all those parents and politicians who have the remotest interest in education. Perhaps, however, it under-emphasizes one point, though it does not ignore it: the difficulty, even within the State system, of integrating newcomers at sixteen in an established community in which all the other pupils have grown up from the age of thirteen. The newcomers are always liable to be resented, particularly because their age and size mean that special account has to be taken of them immediately: they are bound to be in line for positions of authority and for privileges (as were the Swindon boys at Marlborough) and therefore viewed with jealousy by the younger boys who have already 'belonged' for several years. Nor is it easy, in *any* strange school, to adapt quickly to different patterns of authority, of custom, of teaching and learning.

It says much for Marlborough, then, that by the second year one Swindon boy was editing the school magazine, another playing for the school at rugger, a third captain of athletics, and a fourth a successful painter; that eight of the twenty-one became house prefects, and three heads of their houses.

The process of integration would certainly have been easier for the school (though not necessarily for the boys) had it concerned thirteen-year-old boys rather than sixteen-year-olds. The former would have suffered more silently and conformed more readily. But the challenge which the latter group were mature and strong enough to offer was far more salutary. The Lambert-Stagg report has no doubt been carefully studied by every teacher at Marlborough and by many of the older boys too. If it leads (as one hopes it will) to a determination to build on this experience, and to a realization that the next steps must be more radical, this courageous enterprise will have been well worth while.

Two main conclusions are to be drawn from the Marlborough experiment. First, as Lambert makes plain, if integration on a large scale were to be attempted, 'public' school life would be resented and rejected by a big proportion of adolescents from lower-middle and working class homes, accustomed to local schools.

Secondly, in the light of modern psychological and social knowledge, the educational quality of much that is central to the life of the 'public' school is seriously called into question. Ought not the State to require of them fundamental changes before permitting not only children from the State system, but fee-payers themselves, to undergo what most trained educators must find an unsound preparation for living? The responsibility on the Government to face this embarrassing situation is all the greater because the 'public' schools still recruit mainly from the leaders of the community, still see their task as largely the education of future leaders, and still in fact discharge this function. Certainly it would seem that the essential first step in integration would be a widespread exchange of teachers between State and 'public' schools. It would be more effective, and more easily achieved, than the putting of large numbers of local pupils back under the *ancien régime* of educational practice.

The present position is a standing challenge to all who believe that our great need is education for democracy, involving a sensitive respect for private hopes and fears and peculiarities, and putting first and foremost the development of secure and happy people. So the 'public' schools must change or be changed. They have much to give if brought into the mainstream of the nation's educational life. The quickest and most effective way of doing this would seem to be to integrate the teachers first, rather than the children. The implications of such an approach will be considered in my final chapter.

5. A Programme For Progress

A BOOK on comprehensive schools should not use the title at all if it does not, however unworthily, at least attempt to view the subject in a truly comprehensive way. The purpose of our study is to help us to understand the present and to make intelligent decisions about the future. We must, then, look ahead and consider what are likely to be the main issues which will occupy our attention during the next ten years and perhaps beyond.

A reformed system of education

Now that the comprehensive principle has been accepted, critical attention must be given to the shape it is taking in practice. A giant question-mark rears itself against the hotch-potch of schemes for reorganization, which must surely be tidied up when local government is itself re-organized following the Maud report.

A new Education Act must take account of these new factors. The concepts of 'primary' and 'secondary' schooling should probably be abandoned, and replaced by that of compulsory education up to sixteen, whose stages may be indicated by broad suggestions from the Department of Education and Science about the nature of the curriculum to be followed in each. Such stages might well be 5–8, 8–12 and 12–16, though (as in Sweden) they could be differently grouped to meet local needs, e.g. children aged 5–12 might sometimes be in the one school, or 8–16, or (as explained below) 12–18.

The first year of compulsory education should involve only half a day's compulsory attendance, and voluntary half-day schooling before the age of five should be encouraged.

Beyond sixteen we shall have voluntary education, and this will take a great profusion of forms. There will be full-time courses, mainly in colleges of various kinds, but some will continue to be attached to schools. Entry to these courses should be limited only by the student's capacity to profit from them, not by shortage of places – a principle accepted by the Robbins report.[1]

There will also be part-time courses of many kinds, e.g. sandwich, day release, and evening, at every level, including first degrees at universities. A valuable stimulus will be provided by the Open University.

The enormous variety of provision for education beyond sixteen needs to be rationalized, and this can probably best be done under the umbrella of 'the comprehensive university'. After Maud, each area of local government is likely to have at least one university within its boundaries, together with a polytechnic and several colleges of technology, art, education, and perhaps other disciplines. There is already urgent need for more public control of the finance and management of universities (though not of their freedom to teach what they think is right). The university, the colleges and the local education authority need to come together in a federal organization, similar to those which now oversee teacher training, to plan the provision for all post-sixteen education in the region. This overall planning would ensure more efficient use of resources, and the existence of appropriate opportunities for everyone. It would also facilitate the transfer of students from courses in which they were failing, to more suitable courses which at present are often not available within the separate college or university.

In the years ahead we must keep an even more watchful

1. Par. 31: 'We have assumed as an axiom that courses of higher education should be available for all those who are qualified by ability and attainment to pursue them and who wish to do so.'

eye on what is happening inside the schools. Are liberal ideas about the equal worth of all men, which inspire the movement towards the comprehensive schools, being translated into more democratic social structures? Into broader, more wise and human teaching of world history and sociology? Into more careful psychological guidance of each pupil, greater collaboration between teachers and parents? Increasingly, yes; but not as yet in most English schools. This is not to belittle the heroic achievements of the pioneers, whose first job it was to prove that the schools were successful by the traditional standards which the public understood. This they have amply done.

But we cannot be content with that. Indeed, if a comprehensive system came into being which merely hotted up the individual struggle for power, the rat-race for social prestige, it might be better that the reform had never been begun. As a historian I am realist enough to consider this outcome more than a possibility. And yet – man's age-long struggle towards better things, inching his way along like a worm in the soil, proves too that we must each contribute our pitiful little best to this end in our own way, if life is to have any purpose at all. No one who reads this book will ever see the end of the road. All we can hope to do is first to understand the problem, secondly to create our own vision of the right solution, and thirdly to work towards it with all the good means in our power.

I almost wrote 'all means in our power'. But history is full of misguided men and women who, believing that the end justified any means, in the long run damned themselves and their cause by their ruthless actions: Cromwell at Drogheda ... the men of the Inquisition ... Stalin ... And in more subtle ways, too, reform inspired by unworthy motives, achieved by secret negotiation and pressures, itself becomes tainted. The ambitious, dictatorial

Morant[1] stands as a warning to all educational administrators.

What we, as a people, must resolve is that proposals for important changes must be made public long before any decision on them is taken, with ample time allowed for public debate; that full consultation with parents, teachers, and governors should always precede a local authority's decision to go ahead. This does not mean that elected representatives should abandon their right and duty to make the final decision, even an unpopular one; only that all points of view should first be heard. Morally there is everything to be said for free and open persuasion, nothing at all for the secret *coup*. Why fear the light, if our cause is just? *Magna est veritas et praevalebit*.

Independent schools

Just as rationalization is needed within the State schools system and in the jungle of further and higher education, so the position of independent and direct grant schools must be changed to accord with the higher social and educational standards of society in the 1970s. After many years of marking time democracy is once more on the march, and the existence of schools which in some respects offer superior opportunities to a minority of children, at the expense of the whole, is no longer tolerable.

At the beginning of this book I compared England's three-class educational system to a three-lane athletics track with no staggered start. On the inside lane run the favoured seven per cent who attend independent and semi-independent (direct-grant) schools.

What are their advantages? First, independent schools have distinctly smaller classes than the schools run by local authorities. In LEA primary schools in January 1967

1. Sir Robert Morant, Permanent Secretary to the Board of Education, 1903–11.

there were twenty-eight pupils per teacher, and 92,000 of the 138,000 classes had from thirty to fifty or more pupils in each. Grammar schools were slightly better off: there were seventeen pupils per teacher, but 8,000 of the 25,000 classes had more than thirty pupils. Comprehensive schools had eighteen pupils per teacher, and more than one-third of the 15,000 classes had more than thirty pupils.

The picture in recognized independent schools is very different. There, the pupil-to-teacher ratio in primary schools is thirteen, in schools which are primary cum-secondary fourteen, and in secondary schools eleven. The sizes of their classes are not given, but can be deduced. In all the maintained primary and secondary schools of England and Wales there are 318,000 teachers, including allowance for part-timers, and the pupil-to-teacher ratio is twenty-three. In all recognized independent schools the corresponding figures are 24,000 teachers, and a ratio of thirteen. There are other independent schools, not yet recognized as efficient, whose average number of pupils per full-time teacher is fourteen. This category, one hopes, will gradually be eliminated. In direct-grant grammar schools the pupil-to-teacher ratio is fifteen and a half.

Why should independent schools have such material advantages in staffing? One reason is, quite simply, that these schools are prepared to spend more money on teachers than are the Government and local councils. Independent governing bodies tend to believe that teachers are important: more important than buildings and equipment, though they do not despise these things. Where fees and funds permit, they will not only engage a good many more teachers than a local authority school would be allowed to have, but will even pay them more than the national (Burnham) scale.

Parents endorse this line. More and more queue up to pay the ever-rising fees which such a policy requires. Fees at leading schools like Eton, Roedean and Heathfield are around £600 a year or more; at Millfield School, where the pupil-to-teacher ratio is only five, they may rise to £1,000. Some members of the Government and the civil service who each year pare the estimates for national expenditure on education may well at the same time be signing big cheques for the education of their own children or grandchildren at independent schools. This applies to Labour as well as Conservative M.P.s and voters, though the proportion of the former is much smaller.

The danger is clear. Men and women whose children are withdrawn from the old bare buildings of the local primary school, from the strain and hazards of the eleven-plus examination, from the overcrowded classes of the comprehensive or 'secondary modern', are likely to lack some of the urgency which compels reform. Without a doubt, the most valid and powerful argument for bringing all independent schools into the State system is that it would bring the young Macmillans, Hailshams, Snows, and Bonham-Carters into the local classrooms. The chance of early vigorous action to wipe out the black spots in national education would be transformed overnight.

Teachers, too, are quite rare creatures now; there are not nearly enough of them. To prevent attractive resorts like Brighton and Bournemouth enticing more than their share from Birmingham and Bootle, the local authorities observe a rationing scheme – the kind of scheme we found fair and necessary with food, clothes, building materials, petrol, and so on during the 1940s. But in the war years the rich citizen was not legally allowed to buy more than his fair share. Today he can do just that in education, on average buying the services of twice as many teachers for his son at an independent school as a poor man's child will get at a local school.

The power of the purse, used in such a way, must be

ended. It sins against natural justice. In the long run, moreover, it is a time-bomb under the independent schools themselves which could eventually lead to their total abolition.

Three reforms are needed at once. The first is that all independent schools should conform to the corresponding LEA pupil-to-teacher ratio, with a reasonable allowance of extra staff for boarding schools, whether independent or in the State system. The second is that all schools, independent and maintained alike, should pay salaries only according to the Burnham scale, with deductions for benefits such as residence. If a school's reputation and atmosphere attract highly-qualified men well and good; but the rich school should not steal the cream of talent from either the poor independent school or the local authority's school by the clink of money alone. The third, as suggested in the previous chapter, is that there should be a wide and often permanent exchange of teachers between the independent and the State schools; and this should be reinforced by the future recruitment of most independent school staff from men and women who were themselves educated in State schools.

Of course, a period of at least ten years would have to be allowed to enable the relatively over-staffed schools of Eton and Harrow, Winchester and Millfield, to adjust to the new 'fair shares' order without hardship to individual teachers. Even so, the change would bring not insignificant results. The Public Schools Commission has estimated that 'if all recognized schools were staffed to produce the same qualified teacher/pupil ratio (weighted by age of pupils and for boarding pupils) as at present applies in maintained schools . . . there was in 1966 a theoretical "surplus" in recognized schools of 1,532 qualified and 3,434 unqualified teachers'.[1]

1. *First Report* (H.M.S.O., 1968), par. 72.

When these changes are agreed, England will be able to look less passionately at the idea and practice of independent schools. Much could be and has been written, erudite and entertaining, attractive and alarming, about what goes on inside them and what they stand for. The public schools have had their internal as well as external critics, from Alec Waugh to John Wilson.[1] In 1958, a righteously indignant Labour Party roared its denunciation.

This system [it thundered] distorts the choice of people for responsible positions; it damages national efficiency and offends the sense of justice. Further, it creates an irrational social cleavage which is a great injury to education as a whole ... All members of the Labour Party, and indeed all who desire equality of opportunity and social justice, will agree that the existence of this privileged sector of education is undesirable.[2]

But what did it then propose to do about this terrible state of affairs? Nothing whatever. A later conference took a more positive line, but by that time decisions of Labour conferences had ceased to matter as they once did.

The purely educational benefits given by an orthodox boarding school are overrated. Boys and masters live an unnaturally restricted life in a closed, almost monastic community. All the enlightened cultural pursuits that can be devised do not produce the freedom to be either sociable or alone, to be part of the busy life of one's neighbourhood, to belong to home instead of being a stranger in the holidays, that a good day school ensures. The life of the boarding school, in relation to the world of the late twentieth century, is exclusive; that of the day school inclusive. The fact that the Russians have espoused boarding-school education, with its great potential for conditioning its products, is by no means a recommendation.

1. *Public Schools and Private Practice*, 1962.
2. *Learning to Live.*

The essential fact is that the 'public' schools, despite grave limitations, are socially pre-eminent because they are the places where our rulers used to be educated, and by and large still are. Moreover, personal contacts with Oxford and Cambridge colleges still ensure them an undue proportion of places at our leading universities. In November 1961, two out of every three Cabinet ministers were old boys of 'public' schools, particularly of Eton; so were two thirds of the bishops and the justices, and half of the top civil servants. Forty years back, headmasters like Rendall of Winchester made no bones about their aristocratic faith, their belief in leadership by a privileged élite; forty years on, will the message have changed?

English independent schools fall into three main groups, which are poles apart. Within them, however, individual differences are usually outweighed by the resemblance.

First in prestige and influence are the so-called 'public' schools, some 200 in number, whose heads are members of the Headmasters' conference. The real leaders are the bigger, independent boys' boarding schools such as Eton, Harrow, Winchester, Rugby, Clifton, and Charterhouse. A few, like St Paul's are day schools. Girls' 'public' schools are fewer in both number and influence on national life. The left wing of this powerful group is represented by such schools as Bryanston, Abbotsholme, and Gordonstoun. These are moderately progressive, with a reputation for *not* worshipping games and for encouraging liberal opinion, tough physical effort, and sometimes unorthodox teaching methods. Basically they derive from the Boy Scout era, but the choice of Gordonstoun for Prince Charles has no doubt ensured for them an Indian summer.

The second main group, small in number and in patent influence, but yet of real significance in the underflow of educational ideas, is that of the coeducational 'progressive' schools. The most radical and best known is Summerhill, creation of A. S. Neill, a Scotsman who revolted against the thin-lipped puritanism of John Knox still embraced by so many of his countrymen – perhaps in guilty expiation for their quite contradictory worship of Robby Burns. Neill's ideas are essentially in tune with those of great radical thinkers like Rousseau and Dewey, great teachers like Homer Lane and David Wills.

Neill, more than anyone else, has swung teachers' opinion in this country from its old reliance on authority and the cane to hesitant recognition that a child's first need is love, and with love respect for the free growth of his personality : free, that is, from the arbitrary compulsion of elders, and disciplined instead by social experience. The magic of the inspired reformer is there in Neill's books, in his talks to teachers, who still flock to hear him, above all in the absolute sincerity which marks his own school community. Teachers may soon forget high-sounding principles, but they remember the loveless girl who stole again and again; the girl to whom, on each occasion, Neill gave threepence, and after a particularly big theft fourpence – to prove to her, the *sine qua non* before he could begin to help further, that regardless of what she did he was on her side. Today's friendliness between pupil and teacher is probably the greatest difference between the classrooms of 1970 and those of 1930. The change owes much to Neill, and to others in independent coeducational schools who have practised similar principles.

Yet had independent schools been prohibited would Neill ever have been allowed to do, unhindered, what he needed to do? Freedom in education is a first requirement for the establishment and maintenance of a free society. It must be preserved. This means, however, more than an absence of controls; it means having the wherewithal to live freely : money.

Industry has already given substantial sums of money

to certain independent schools, but a general allocation to all the needy and worthy is required. This can only be provided by the nation as a whole. A fund administered by an independent body, quite detached from the Department of Education and Science, may be the only practicable arrangement. Part of its financial responsibility would be the support of children whose need for boarding education has been established by an appropriate professional committee. It will work so long as we as a people favour liberal principles; and if we lose them, freedom inside or outside the State system of schools will not survive.

The third main group of independent schools is a mixed bag of minor boarding schools (preparatory and secondary) and small independent day schools, usually for younger children. Too many of these exist because of social snobbery, a desire that 'nice' children shall not mix with street kids and learn naughty words, rough accents, and bad manners. (These same parents go dutifully to church to pay their respects to the memory of a man whose personal example was that of mixing with the riff-raff.) Other parents choose them because they want the advantage of small classes for their children, and are prepared to buy these superior conditions, though in the long run this is done at the expense of other children.

I have urged that independent schools should be preserved, but that material privileges should not be bought there; and further, that there should be no social segregation of teachers as between State and independent schools. With these provisions enforced, we may expect most of the unworthy schools to wither away. What we ought not to destroy is the distinctive character, perhaps the spiritual atmosphere, of schools with a truly educational purpose. The freedom of Summerhill and Dartington is matched by the Anglican worship of Clifton, by Catholic Stonyhurst, Quaker Ackworth, and Methodist Kingswood.

All have their special contributions to make to a free, classless, diversified, creative society. None of these schools should choose, or I think would choose, to gather to itself only the most able, the naturally favoured children. Each should be a mixed comprehensive community, taking children who for one reason or another cannot have a normal home and school upbringing.

In sum, we need to weed out the worst of the independent schools, to keep and in some respects reform the best. That done, independent schools – along with aided schools of similar foundation – will become a necessary part of a full system of comprehensive education. Without them a free society would be incomplete.

Direct grant grammar schools

Poised uneasily between the State system and the independent schools, this comparative handful (178) of highly selective academic schools represent a philosophy which is completely opposite to that which has brought about comprehensive reorganization. It is widely accepted that their unsatisfactory position must be ended, and that such schools should have the choice either of going independent, and thus losing the financial support from the State which they now enjoy, or coming under the local education authority.

Few of the direct grant schools have sufficient funds to enable them to assume independent status, and unless the comprehensive tide is held back by a change of political control at Westminster it must be assumed that almost all will before long become schools maintained by the local education authority and therefore absorbed in whatever form of comprehensive organization is favoured locally. The basic issue is a simple one, and it is unfortunate from the point of view of both the schools and the local education authority that a decision on these lines was not made quickly by the Labour Government and incorporated in the advice given in Circular 10/65.

Schools for the community

Home is the baby's world. For all other members of the family, however, it is not sufficient in itself, though essential as a fount of love and security. Both children and parents need a much richer, more varied social life than modern homes – little brick huts in lonely suburban streets – can give. In each neighbourhood we need not only people sharing a whole range of occupations, but as much as possible the places where those occupations are carried on. The segregation of 'residential areas' from factories, shops, and offices betrays an abysmal ignorance of social psychology.

At the same time we must make the best of the actual situation today. We have to recognize that the need for a planned extension of educational facilities is made more urgent by the cultural poverty of the urban and suburban street, and by the latter's lack of communal life. In this situation we cannot overlook the example of Peckham. Between 1926 and 1950 the Pioneer Health Centre at Peckham, one of the inner suburbs of south-east London, showed in impressive fashion what could be done.

The Peckham centre had a medical wing, swimming bath, gymnasium, canteen, theatre, library, and a range of rooms which could be adapted for different social activities. It also had its own nursery and primary school. Membership was limited to whole families from the immediate neighbourhood – the distance that a woman could push a pram. It was essentially an experiment in the positive promotion of social health, in the enrichment of the physical and cultural life of a mixed community; and it ended, ironically enough, when this formerly self-supporting centre, hit by steeply rising costs after the war, failed to get financial support from a Labour Government pledged to the advancement of social welfare.

Its example remains, though no community centre so complete has yet been developed elsewhere. The need for a stronger link between school and home at the primary stage is particularly important.

Nursery-infant schools are wanted, for they help enormously to widen a child's social experience. There he is safe, busy, and happy. The school can provide play material specially designed for his use. The teachers are trained to understand his needs. Above all, in these days of small families, he has there the companionship necessary for his proper social and emotional development.

Instead of full-time schooling from five to six as at present, the young child needs to be initiated gradually into the exhausting social life of school. At the same time there is no doubt that a great many four-year-old children are fretfully at a loose end while at home. The sensible answer is to introduce half-time schooling, voluntary at four, compulsory at five. It would make no extra demands on either our buildings or our supply of teachers. By local arrangement, and taking into account as far as possible mothers' preferences, each child would attend school either in the morning (9.30–12 noon) or the afternoon (1.30–4.0). Some children would stay for school dinner after the morning session, others would come for it before the afternoon session. More would have dinner at home, but the extra age-group would probably mean that the total having school dinner aged from four to six would not differ very much from the number aged five to six who now have it.

School should not, however, be a means of taking the child *from* the mother or of relieving her of responsibility. We are paying far more than an economic price for the labour of married women. We pay with the neglect of small children while mother and father are away from home, with insecurity and personal and social instability. One supports both people's need for a higher standard of living and the need of most married women for a fuller social life. Yet if we really believe that proper attention and security in early childhood are essential for later happiness and the prevention of delinquency, we ought to forbid the *full-time* employment of mothers whose children are under six years old, at least; and we should bear the economic consequences. If history is any guide at all, necessity would produce the appropriate solution – most probably a speeding-up of automation.

It would of course be wrong and futile to do no more than order women back to the kitchen. The necessary complement is to develop our primary schools as social and education centres for children *and mothers*. They could be very simple versions of Peckham. Attached to the school would be a small branch of the county library, with books and magazines of special interest to mothers. The weekly clinic would be held in a suitable room on the premises. An attractively furnished canteen-cum-common room could be run by the staff who provide school dinners; indeed, any further use of existing capital plant (in this case the kitchens) should always be welcomed as contributing to greater efficiency and economy. Talks and discussions could be arranged occasionally in mornings or afternoons for mothers whose children were in school at the same time. This is an idea which Townswomen's Guilds, Women's Institutes, and Mothers' Unions might well consider.

Something of the kind is already being done, as we have seen, at the Lawrence Weston School, and also at one or two colleges of education. On one half-day a week more than a score of local mothers may bring their children of pre-school age, including babies, to the nursery-infant department or the pre-school play group. Students look after the children while mothers play tennis, keep fit on the trampoline, study flower arrangements, or paint. Experts from big stores give talks on such topics as fashions and make-up. The local health visitor may talk about child management. These mothers greatly value their visits.

Such a solution would seem to take account of all the main points which at present cause us concern: the need to initiate young children gradually, instead of frightening them by pushing them in off the deep end; the need to enlarge and enrich the social life of young mothers, without driving them away from their families to factory, office, or shop; the need to divert our growing national wealth to the areas of society where its support is most needed; and finally, the very practical need to achieve these reforms without making any extra demands on the already insufficient supply of teachers, and with a minimum of extra building.

We should then look forward to a ten-year period of full-time comprehensive schooling for everyone, from six to sixteen. Throughout this period our schools must be ready to feed and provide for children's special interests as they emerge. We should reject any notion of a completely uniform curriculum which would put them all in a straitjacket. There are precious talents of language and music, art and drama, for example, which will sometimes require extra time; and in the later years, at least, a boy or girl may have good reason to drop some subject or subjects and to concentrate more thoroughly on others. Just as emphatically, we must stop forcing children to choose one subject to the exclusion of another, before they want or are ready to make that choice.

The question is often posed: should a school prepare a pupil to fit into existing society or to change it? For me the choice does not arise. Society will change in any case –

all living things do. The important question is: in what direction should it change? It is not for any schoolmaster to provide the answer. His job is to help his pupils to open their minds, to gain the experience from which in due course they will be able to think out their own answers.

For that reason I believe the comprehensive school, a school which sets out more specifically than any other to provide for a complete community, should have a special concern to educate its pupils for active participation in a free democracy. It can only do this by letting them work and live in a society which is as democratic as the law of education and the incomplete maturity of the pupils permit. Such a qualification must leave room for considerable disagreement about what is possible and desirable, and it would be wrong for any conservative-minded teacher to budge from his principles. Sincerity on his part ensures security for the child. Nevertheless, there is room for a much greater degree of democracy than is common in England's schools. For this reason the example being set by a growing number of the pioneer comprehensive schools is particularly welcome.

The principle need of modern democracy is not that we should pick or train a class of leaders whom the rest can follow with unquestioning loyalty, but that we should spread responsibility much more widely and encourage intelligent discussion and active participation in councils and committees by everyone. Enlargement must replace selection, socially as well as in the curriculum.

Each group situation will produce its own Admirable Crichton to take charge when required, provided an officially-appointed élite does not already sit in the seat of power. There should be many groupings of various sizes within a school. A small group can act as a whole. When it is too large to do this, authority can often be delegated *ad hoc* for particular purposes to different people. In this way, every boy and girl receives some training in democratic procedure, and a large proportion of them are likely to hold executive office for a time. The extension of personal experience is essential to the effective working of a democratic system. We want all, not only a favoured or ambitious few, to become active citizens in the future.

Why do so many heads, of all types of school, hesitate about this vitally important aspect of the social education of their pupils? Some, perhaps, are not well informed of experiments elsewhere, and it does not occur to them to adopt any system other than that to which they have been accustomed. There may be an element of caution; it is easier and safer to appoint your own agents than to risk having to work with individuals appointed by others, and of whom you may not approve. Moreover, it greatly strengthens a headmaster's hand to wield this power of patronage. 'All power corrupts . . .' and where is the tyrant who has voluntarily become a constitutional monarch? It is easier and more efficient to take decisions quickly than to await the laborious processes of committees – especially when you know the answer much better than they. 'Democracy only rates two cheers', as E. M. Forster observed, even with the man in the street. It can hardly be expected to evoke an eager welcome from the average headmaster's chair. Education in democracy requires the guidance of mature, relaxed, patient men and women, who are not plagued with subconscious doubts about themselves, the children, or the rightness of the policy they are carrying out.

The secondary schools, whatever their age range, have a job to do which extends far beyond the classroom and the individual pupils. I have suggested that the primary school should be a social and educational centre for children and mothers too. But the family does not cease to exist when childhood gives way to adolescence. Marriage-guidance councillors tell us that marriages are most in danger after the first ten years. Every member of the family, mother and father, boy and girl, feels the pressing call for a fuller, more satisfying life than the ordinary home can possibly provide by itself. The cleavage of each from the others is not uncommon, yet Peckham showed that it need not happen.

The secondary school which serves the whole local community is the nucleus around which a rich and happy neighbourhood life can be built. It must be more than a school: rather, a community college on the Cambridgeshire and Leicestershire models. It should be a centre of local culture, entertainment, and recreation. Its premises should be available to whatever societies may spring up. There must be games rooms, comfortably furnished common rooms, playing fields, library, and all the appurtenances of a civilized and very diverse community of people. Not least of the dividends will be the recognition that the school is but part of a larger whole, that parents belong there too, that the whole business of education is a matter for consultation among the interested parties – parents, teachers, adult tutors, committee members, and so on. A Dr Busby would hardly be an appropriate appointment for the wardenship of such a democratic institution.

The sixth-form college

What of the sixth form? It is important that at this stage, with academically minded pupils and teachers, we retain the attitudes of scholarship which distinguish the best grammar, comprehensive, and independent schools. The two last-named types of school have exploded the fallacy that these attitudes can only be created with a segregated academic élite. The comprehensive schools are already attracting increasing numbers of sixteen-to-eighteen-year-olds who want courses which, whether general or geared to future careers in industry or commerce, must be quite different from those of the Oxbridge scholarship hunter.

There are powerful arguments in favour of providing for the older adolescent in separate sixth-form colleges. Support for this arrangement, first canvassed during the 1940s, is now rapidly gaining ground. Today we have not only the independent Atlantic College and the Mexborough experiment, but also colleges already established at Luton and elsewhere, and plans for more throughout the country.[1]

The advantages of the sixth-form college are these. First, such a community, of moderate size (say 300–500), can yet economically and efficiently offer a more varied programme than that available in the vast majority of grammar- and comprehensive-school sixth forms. Expensive advanced equipment can be provided, in the knowledge that it will be fully used. Highly-qualified specialist staff will likewise be employed to maximum advantage.

Secondly, it would be possible in such a college to treat the pupils as students, giving them a bigger share in the running of their own community than is normally possible in school. They would feel that they had left school behind, and the prospect of meeting and working with sixth-formers drawn from other schools would be an attractive one. We need to widen adolescent horizons, not restrict them. It may be felt that the idea of 'staying on at school' is irksome to many, particularly sixteen-year-old girls, and that the routine duties of patrolling corridors and keeping younger children in order are not very impressive forms of training in responsibility. As others leave, the sixth-former may feel he is becoming a bigger and bigger fish in an ever-dwindling pond.

In the college, on the other hand, he would mix with

1. See Appendix.

many more sixth-formers from a variety of schools. This would enlarge his social experience and give him a different sort of responsibility, akin to that of the university undergraduate. Indeed, I feel that sixth-formers are ready for the degree of self-government hitherto accorded to university students today, and that the latter in turn ought – as they have begun so forcibly to demand – to be treated much more like adults than fledglings.

In some rural areas, houses for weekly boarders would be necessary. The experience would do many country children a world of good. In their late teens they need to get away more than they do from their rather isolated homes. This gentle easing of the bonds would be a valuable experience.

Thirdly, although some grammar schools let their brighter pupils by-pass the ordinary-level examinations of GCE and go on to specialist sixth-form work early, the great majority of schools still prefer to give a general education to fifteen or sixteen and put their pupils in for a broad range of ordinary-level subjects. This is partly because parents, pupils, and teachers like to have an external guide to the pupil's best future course of study; but it is also a partial guarantee against premature specialization.

Beyond the ordinary level of GCE, teachers commonly adopt a different, a tutorial approach to their pupils. This is the best feature of grammar-school education; and in many places, as the demand for higher education spreads strongly, the logical arrangement is to ask an existing grammar school to concentrate increasingly and eventually wholly on sixth-form work with students aged fifteen or sixteen to eighteen-plus. There is an excellent precedent in Sweden's *gymnasium*, with its fifteen-to-nineteen age range. This would, for example, be a logical and attractive next step in Leicestershire, where upper schools for four-teen-year-olds to eighteen-year-olds are over-full, while junior high schools, at present doing only the groundwork for GCE up to fourteen, are perfectly capable of providing for all up to sixteen, including ordinary-level work.

By this arrangement those pupils who will leave at sixteen, and they are likely for some time to be the majority, can take a leading part in their school's affairs to an extent impossible while they are overshadowed by sixth-formers.

The fact is that schools, like the people of whom they are composed, tend to grow up. The grammar school's normal age range was at one time eight to sixteen. Since the war it has become eleven to eighteen. It is realistic to ask 'modern' and grammar schools to stop pretending that they are equal and parallel and to start functioning end-on.

The comprehensive college of further education

So far I have said nothing about the people who will still leave as early as sixteen even when compulsory schooling is extended for an extra year. Crowther held out only the most distant hopes of the introduction of part-time county colleges for those aged from sixteen to eighteen; yet since 1944, in theory and in statute, we have recognized the need to extend educational guidance to eighteen for everyone. The 1944 Education Act prescribed county colleges which would give compulsory education for one day per week for forty-four weeks in the year, or, with rural districts in mind, one term of eight weeks or two terms of four weeks each. The Crowther council felt that this must come after the raising of the leaving age. Meanwhile, it encouraged the extension of day-release courses at colleges of further education. Between 1970 and 1980 it was hoped to have five years' experience with compulsory part-time attendance in a few chosen areas, followed by its gradual extension over the whole country.

All these plans for compulsory part-time general education now seem likely to come to naught, although the Industrial Training Act is bringing more and more young people back for vocational courses. The provision of separate colleges for part-timers only, as envisaged in the 1944 Act, has proved very difficult in practice, and this explains why we have shied away from tackling the problem. It would be hard to find yet more sites for educational buildings in urban centres. Further, the total number of pupils the staff of such a college must handle is too great, as we know from the experience of existing day-continuation colleges like Bournville and Boots. Four hundred students a day means 2,000 a week – far too many for the staff to get to know well; yet close personal knowledge and influence are more important than anything else to teenagers. Nor is it easy to see how staff of the high calibre necessary would be recruited for such work alone.

A much more likely development is the comprehensive college for all aged from fifteen or sixteen to eighteen-plus. This would be a development of the process for which I have reasoned already; the transformation of the grammar school into a school or college for older adolescents.

We are already finding that comprehensive schools have to provide for a new type of sixth-former – the boy or girl who is not at all academic. To this extent the cleavage between students and others is blurred, and socially this is all to the good. But the parting of the ways between the scholar, the professional man, and the educated technician on the one side, all of whom are in future likely to stay at school to eighteen, and the unskilled or semi-skilled young worker on the other, who leaves at sixteen or earlier, is still sharp. They take different roads into adult life, and it is in late adolescence that impressions burn deepest. There is a very real danger that, despite comprehensive schooling to sixteen, this sharp divergence of experience and interests thereafter will undermine at least some of the good foundations laid earlier; and that in later life, class differences and lack of mutual understanding will be almost as strong as ever they were.

The new kind of sixth form in comprehensive schools is the first sign of a familiar historical process. A higher range of education for older pupils, first appreciated by the wealthy and the able, is gradually coming to seem desirable to more and more of the working class. This process will go on; but as we go down the scale of natural ability, post-sixteen education will have to include a considerable amount of practical work. Such work must be realistic – and where better can a good apprenticeship be given than in an up-to-date factory or office? One can foresee the development of very close links between the sixth-form college and industry, just as in a different sphere one can expect much closer collaboration between college and school in the training of teachers.

The Russians are beginning to realize the importance of mixing studies with practical work in the later teens. We too are questioning excessive specialization, and feeling the need to develop rounded people, whole men. More time is being spent by intellectual sixth-formers on arts and crafts and technical jobs. Leicester's Gateway School is a splendid example of this. The trend will continue. As it does, the distinction between continuing one's education and going out to work will fade. More and more pupils will opt for the former when it is seen as a realistic all-round education with a vocational point to it. It has always had such a point for the future lawyer, teacher, or administrator; we shall merely be extending it to the more varied needs of all members of society.

It does not take any great effort of the imagination, then, to visualize the sixth-form college of the future as pretty comprehensive in the range of activities it offers and the

range of ability it attracts. It will be staffed by some of the
most gifted personalities in the teaching profession, men
and women who by achievement and character can win
the regard of critical sixteen- to eighteen-year-old pupils.
Its academic prowess will ensure high prestige in the community at large. Economically it will be the soundest of
propositions, by intensive use fully justifying first-rate
staffing and equipment.

It may well be, then, that instead of the cumbersome
arrangements which formal compulsory part-time education would always require, the really practical answer will
lie in the process with which we are already familiar:
the voluntary extension of education, clinched in due
course by the government's compulsion, to ensure that the
children of poor or obtuse parents are not left for ever
out in the cold. So we should simply have compulsory education extended first to seventeen and ultimately perhaps
to eighteen.

The great difference between past and future extensions,
however, must be this. In the past we have talked, rightly,
of 'raising the school-leaving age'. In future we must
speak of 'college education for all'. The new phrase implies near-adult status and freedom, and optional courses
of study. It implies, too, a very flexible administration
which will make it possible for some students to have four
days at their books and one in the workshop, others four
days in the factory (a good well-run one) and one at their
books, and others again varying proportions of study and
practical work in between those extremes.

Of course we need a national overhaul of apprenticeship
systems. A survey in December 1961 by the Institute of
Youth Employment Officers showed that many employers
misuse the term 'apprenticeship' and fail to provide adequate training. The concept of apprenticeship is a splendid
thing, but the time has come for it to be placed firmly

under the wing of the local education authority. Grants in lieu of wages might well be made to students who chose to attend the college beyond sixteen – an excellent and just way of helping the desired development in the early, voluntary stage.

The term 'sixth form' is too limited and inappropriate for an institution of the kind I have been describing. 'Junior college' would be even more patronizing and inept. The sensible term would surely be simply 'county college': dignified and pleasing to the ear, and symbolic of the importance of our local education authorities in the national system of education. Its part-time connotation is already something of a dead letter.

Most appealing and practical of all, perhaps, is the proposal that both full-time and part-time education beyond sixteen should become the responsibility of existing colleges of further education. The extent of the work they now do in this field is not generally realized: in 1966 no fewer than 687,000 students aged 15–20 were receiving day-time education in these colleges, of whom 144,000 were full-time students. They have plenty of experience of GCE Ordinary and Advanced level work, and are successful with many students who come to them in despair after failing these examinations at school.

The facilities offered by the colleges of further education are more wide-ranging than is possible in any school sixth form. The false distinction between academic and vocational studies naturally disappears, and it is possible to provide more precisely for the different needs of the individual student. The Civic College at Ipswich, for example, has hundreds of full-time students drawn from secondary schools and admitted without examination on the head teacher's recommendation. A wide range of subjects is offered to GCE 'O' and 'A' levels. Some students go on to universities and colleges of education, others stay at the Civic College and qualify in art, engineering, building, clerical and secretarial work, and so on.

Socially the colleges of further education have considerable attractions for the growing number of older adolescents who feel restricted by the regimen of school, by rules and customs which have been designed with children in mind. At the same time they do not cut off this age-group from older students as does a separate sixth-form college; and since the period 16–19 can be no more than an introduction to adulthood the continuity in the social life and attitudes of a college which can add rather more maturity is to be welcomed. It is not surprising to find that further education students often behave in a more responsible, indeed 'grown-up', way than do first-year university students recruited straight from school sixth forms.

Finally, these colleges have proved their ability to weave full-time and part-time education together in one community. When they are allowed to provide for everyone over sixteen the richness of the life and studies of such a truly comprehensive community will become notable indeed.

It is with such considerations in mind that two local education authorities in the South-West of England, acting quite separately, have decided on plans to provide comprehensive secondary schools up to sixteen and to concentrate all education beyond sixteen in the local college of further education: one in the city of Exeter, the other (under Devon County Council) at Barnstaple in North Devon. At the time of writing both schemes, however, await the approval of the Department of Education and Science.

The real future of the comprehensive idea does not, then, lie in the comprehensive secondary school as it is at present understood. It has been an invaluable pioneer, experimental, intermediate institution. The schools of Leicestershire, having taken us further on the way, must in turn develop, or hand over the torch. Given the will, we can shape all our existing schools, colleges and universities into a vigorous, national, comprehensive system.

The teachers

Comprehensive education does more than open the doors of opportunity to all children. It represents a different, a larger and more generous attitude of mind. For fifty years we have been too preoccupied with the mere *measurement* of ability; with testing and grading, with selection and rejection and allocation. Many teachers and administrators have almost come to regard this classification as their main job. Worshipping at an altar bearing the mystic symbol 'I.Q.', set up by a priesthood of pseudo-scientists called 'psychometrists', they have sometimes seemed to forget the age-old power of teaching, and the capacity of a child to keep on growing and learning – when it is put in the right environment.

Now our teachers, in all types of school, are beginning to turn from the false gods, to concern themselves less with the arid assessment of a child's inborn ability and idle predictions about its future ceiling, and more with nourishing all the diverse talents children children have. I say, deliberately, that this is a fresh approach – not a new approach : for it is truly a rebirth of learning, not a revolution in education. Those who protest so vigorously against present trends, and describe them as an assault on traditional values, need a historical perspective which goes a little further back than War Office selection boards.

If the comprehensive schools are to take full advantage of the reforms which are afoot in the framework of our system, they need above all broad-minded scholarly teachers who see themselves as friends and counsellors rather than as circus-masters, who rely on timely advice and encouragement rather than the superficial incentives of the whip and the carrot. If we turn back the pages of history we can often catch a glimpse of what first-class teaching quality can do.

From 1796 to 1833 Richmond School, Yorkshire, had only from fifty to sixty boys each year; but under a great scholar and master, James Tate, five or six went every year to either Cambridge or Oxford. Half of them took Firsts; no less than thirteen of 'Tate's Invincibles', as they were called, were elected fellows of Trinity, and more became fellows elsewhere. Such was the pride and confidence of Richmond in its little school that every year, when the Cambridge tripos results were due, the whole town turned out, gathering round the Market Cross to await the coming of the carrier up the Great North Road with his news of yet more triumphs.[1]

But the Tates, the Thrings, the Arnolds are all too rare; and with less-gifted masters Richmond faded into obscurity. Today, while we rejoice in the 'ups', we cannot afford to contemplate such 'downs' as overtook our forebears in the eighteenth and nineteenth centuries. We need a high and constant level of competence to sustain the brilliant; and that means training. If university standards of scholarship and quality are to pervade our comprehensive schools, both primary and secondary, it can best be done through university institutes and faculties of education which bring together all concerned in the education of teachers – universities, colleges, teachers' associations, local education authorities, and the Department of Education and Science – on an equal footing in a cooperative group.

We have today a deeply divided teaching profession. Only one teacher in three in maintained secondary schools

1. L. P. Wenham, *The History of Richmond School, Yorkshire* (Herald Press, 1958).

is a graduate; only one in twenty-five in maintained primary schools. In recognized independent schools the corresponding figures are four out of five and one in three. To four out of five of all teachers in maintained schools, university scholarship is a closed book; and they have never experienced the rich variety of contacts with able minds geared to widely different interests. Their world has been the comparatively narrow world of the training college – a world of teachers and would-be teachers only, with its legacy of inferior conditions and staffing ratios, an out-of-date relic of the old elementary system.

Is it possible for an all-round improvement in the general education of our people to be achieved, if the mental nourishment and stimulation of teachers themselves is to be cramped in this way? It is not enough to modify and improve training-college conditions, important and desirable as are the steps being taken to this end.

Equally unacceptable is the argument that most primary teachers and some secondary teachers are unsuited to an academic university course. This overlooks the pre-war position, when it was common to have in our universities men whose ability and attainment were no greater than those of most of the students now in training colleges; yet they gave much to the life of the university community and gained much from it.

The truth is that only the best education is good enough for the teachers of the prosperous society that will be the Britain of the future, a Britain relying more than ever before on trained intelligence for its prosperity. That means a university education now for all who can profit by it; and ultimately, as overall standards steadily rise, for all teachers.

The day is coming, and the sooner the better, when all graduates who wish to teach in school are required first of all to train. It would, however, be a great mistake if we followed Scotland in taking the professional education and training of teachers out of the universities, instead of seeking integration the other way by bringing it all in. The Scottish 'colleges of education' are still conscious of their inferior status *vis-à-vis* the universities, and many concerned with their work and government now favour their incorporation in neighbouring universities. I have observed this process of integrating training colleges in the universities of Canada at different stages in different provinces, and I am convinced that it is both right and feasible. The new 'college and faculty of education' must be regarded as roughly equivalent in size, and fully equal in status, not to another department (e.g. of history, or classics, or botany) but to the faculty of arts, or science, or social science, or medicine.

It is essential, at the earliest possible moment, to require all graduates who wish to teach to train for the job. It is also necessary to make the new B.Ed. degree more relevant to the work of teachers, and so encourage those college students who wish and are suitably qualified to read for it to do so. The B.Ed. degree must also be made available to the thousands of teachers who can only take it by part-time study.

I have suggested earlier that the comprehensive school should be deeply concerned to help to shape and transmit a communal culture, rich and diverse as the colours of rainbow silk, whose essentials all members of a liberal, democratic society can recognize and share. This task is impossible so long as our teachers are themselves sharply divided into what are in effect two classes, graduate and non-graduate, with their different backgrounds and correspondingly different social status and public esteem. The ending of this cleavage is one of the major reforms necessary for the effective development of a system of comprehensive education.

Conclusion

'Nothing', said Victor Hugo, 'is so powerful as an idea whose time has come.'

The case against a divided system of education gains daily in strength. The nation has emphatically rejected the eleven-plus examination and all it has stood for. Discontent over the eighteen-plus bottleneck, which stems from the same restrictive attitudes among those in power, will become still more vocal.

With regard to examination results, comprehensive schools are already spiking the guns of those who raised alarm about the threat to academic standards. Despite the serious handicaps imposed on them, these schools are beginning to suggest that it is the segregated system whose performance was inadequate. Some self-important moguls of education, who take for granted the inferiority of the mass of their fellow men, still cling to their mean gloomy belief in a limited pool of ability, as though the human mind were something static. In fact its capacity for growth is written large on the pages of history. Our pioneer comprehensive schools are nobly adding to that story.

Their continued success, which I confidently expect, will produce a growing flood of young people eager to continue their studies beyond the secondary stage. With the early achievements of these schools in mind, I presented to the Home Universities Conference in 1958 a case for expanding the number of university places in Britain from 124,000, the target then accepted by the University Grants Committee, to a minimum of 170,000 by 1966. This figure was subsequently accepted by the University Grants Committee; and in turn the targets set by the Robbins Committee on Higher Education (219,000 in 1973–4 and 346,000 in 1980–81) are clearly going to be insufficient

– indeed the 1973–4 figure has already been revised upwards.

Looking further ahead, it is impossible to put any ceiling to future expansion. The process of education is self-perpetuating, and the whole record of history indicates that increased opportunity begets ever-increasing response.

At a time when man's resources are greater than ever before, we need correspondingly to think big, to recapture some of the fire and vision of giants like H. G. Wells, Bernard Shaw, Gilbert Murray, and W. T. Stead. 'Moral eunuchs', Stead called those who were afraid to put right what all the evidence showed to be wrong. The term, scathing as it is, would not be out of place in some parts of the education service today. So far we have barely scratched the surface of necessary reform. Today's experiments are but stumbling footsteps on the long road to universal education, which, as Wells prophesied, will be 'organized upon a scale and of a penetration and quality beyond all present experience', and give 'a yield beyond comparison greater than any yield of able and brilliant men that the world has known hitherto'.

Large changes in the framework of our educational system are required, but in themselves they can do no more than make good education possible. They simply get us to the starting-gate. What matters most of all is what goes on inside the schools.

It is very important that our comprehensive schools shall not content themselves with merely achieving equal opportunity for the competitive success of individual pupils. In the years ahead, now that the folly of eleven-plus segregation is everywhere being recognized, they will be tempted of the devil. They will be shown and offered all the scholastic kingdoms, including Oxford and Cambridge, York and Canterbury. Tempting though such prizes are, they must not be allowed to divert the new schools from their larger purpose: the forging of a communal culture by the pursuit of quality with equality, by the education of their pupils in and for democracy, and by the creation of happy, vigorous, local communities in which the school is the focus of social and educational life.

English society in the sixties was far from noble or inspiring. But man is not a helpless creature. It is up to us to direct new forces in the way we believe to be right. 'How much is still alive in England!' cried Carlyle. 'How much has not yet come into life!' But a promise, too, is there: 'The centuries are big; and the birth-hour is coming, not yet come.'

Appendix

PROGRESS IN THE REORGANIZATION OF
SECONDARY EDUCATION (DECEMBER 1968)[1]

(A) *Authorities with schemes approved for all through schools* (85)

Authority	Age Range
Anglesey	11–18
Barnet*	11–18
Barrow-in-Furness	11–18
Barking	11–18
Berkshire*	11–16/11–18
Blackburn*	11–18
Blackpool	11–16/11–18
Bradford*	11–18 s.t.
†Breconshire	11–16/11–18
Brent*	11–18 s.t.
Bristol	11–18
Bromley	11–16/11–18
Burnley*	11–16/11–18 s.t.
†Cambridgeshire*	11–16/11–18
Cardiff*	11–16/16–18
Cardiganshire*	11–18
†Caernarvonshire	11–18
Carlisle	11–18
†Carmarthenshire	11–18
†Cheshire	11–18
Cornwall*	11–18
Coventry	11–18
Croydon*	11–16
Cumberland*	11–18
Darlington*	11–16/11–18
Denbighshire	11–18

* appears also in another category.

s.t. short term only.

† approved scheme covers only part of the area.

1. I am indebted to the Department of Education and Science for this information.

Authority	Age Range
†Derbyshire*	11–18
Devon*	11–18
†Dorset*	11–18
Dudley	11–18
†Ealing	11–18
Eastbourne*	11–16
†Essex	11–16/11–18
Flintshire	11–18
†Glamorgan	11–18
†Gloucestershire	11–16/11–18
†Hampshire*	11–16/11–18
Haringey	11–18
Hartlepools	11–18
Havering	11–18
Herefordshire*	11–16/11–18
Hertfordshire*	11–18
Hounslow*	11–18
Huddersfield*	11–16
Huntingdon and Peterborough	11–16/11–18
Isles of Scilly	11–16
Lancashire*	11–16/11–18
Lincolnshire (Lindsey)*	11–16/11–18
†Lincolnshire (Kesteven)	11–18
†Liverpool	11–16/11–18
†London (I.L.E.A)	11–18
Luton*	11–16
Manchester	11–18
Merioneth	11–18
Merthyr Tydfil	11–18
Montgomeryshire	11–18
†Monmouthshire	11–18
Newcasle upon Tyne	11–18
Newham	11–18
Newport*	11–18
†Northamptonshire*	11–18
Norwich*	11–18
Nottinghamshire*	11–16/11–18
Oldham	11–16/11–18
Oxfordshire	11–18

* appears also in another category.
† approved scheme covers only part of the area.

Authority	Age Range
†Pembrokeshire	11–16/11–18
Preston*	11–16
†Radnorshire	11–18
Rotherham*	11–16
†Shropshire*	11–16/11–18
Solihull	11–18
†Somerset*	11–18
South Shields	11–18
St Helens*	11–18
†Staffordshire	11–18
Sunderland	11–18
Sussex East	11–18
Sussex West	11–18
†Swansea	11–18
Tynemouth*	11–16
Warwickshire*	11–16/11–18
†Wiltshire*	11–16/11–18
West Bromwich*	11–16/11–18
Yorkshire East Riding	11–18
Yorkshire West Riding*	11–16/11–18

(B) *Authorities with middle school systems approved* (40)

Authority	Age Range
Bedfordshire*	9–13
Birkenhead	8–12
Bradford*	9–13
Cumberland*	10–13
Dewsbury*	8–12
Doncaster	9–13
Dorset*	9–13
Great Yarmouth	9–13
Grimsby	8–12
†Hampshire*	8–12
Haringey*	9–13 (C. of E. only)
Hastings	8–12
Herefordshire*	9–13
Hertfordshire*	9–13
Isle of Wight	9–13

* appears also in another category.

† approved scheme covers only part of the area.

Authority	Age Range
Kent	9–13
Kingston upon Hull	9–13
Lancashire* Division 13	9–13
Lincoln County Borough*	8–12
Lincolnshire (Holland)	9–13
Merton	9–13
Northampton County Borough	9–13
Northamptonshire*	9–13/10–13
Northumberland	9–13
Norwich*	8–12
Oxford County Borough	9–13
Sheffield	8–12
†Shropshire*	9–13
†Somerset*	9–13
Southampton	8–12
Stoke on Trent	8–12
Suffolk West*	9–13
Suffolk East*	9–13
†Surrey	9–13
Sussex West*	10–13
Wallasey	9–13
Warwickshire*	9–13
Worcestershire	9–13
York County Borough	9–13
Yorkshire West Riding*	9–13

(C) *Authorities with two-tier arrangements approved* (37)

Authority	Age Range
Barnet*	11–14/14–18
Barnsley	11–14/14–18
Berkshire*	11–14/14–18
Blackburn*	11–14/14–18
Bradford*	11–13/13–16/13–18
Brent*	11–13/13–18 s.t.
Burnley*	11–16/13–18 s.t.
Cardiganshire*	11–13/13–18
†Caernarvonshire*	11–13/13–18

    *   appears also in another category.
s.t.   short term only.
    †   approved scheme covers only part of the area.

Authority	Age Range
†Cambridgeshire*	11–16/13–18 s.t.
	11–14/14–18
Croydon*	11–14/14–18
Cumberland*	11–13/13–16/13–18
†Derbyshire*	11–14/14–18
Devon*	11–14/14–18
†Dorset*	11–14/14–18
Doncaster*	11–16/13–18 s.t.
Enfield	11–14/14–18
Gateshead	11–14/14–18
Hounslow*	11–14/14–18
Huntingdon and Peterborough*	11–14/14–18
Isle of Wight*	11/13/13–16/18 s.t.
†Kent*	11–16/14–18 s.t.
†Lancashire*	11–14/14–18
	11–13/11–16/13–18
Leicestershire	11–14/14–18
Liverpool*	11–14/14–18 s.t.
Middlesbrough	11–16/13–18
Newport*	11–13/13–16/18 s.t.
†Northamptonshire*	11–13/13–18
	11–14/14–18 s.t.
Northampton County Borough*	11–16/13–18 s.t.
Nottinghamshire*	11–13/13–16/13–18
Oxfordshire*	11–14/14–18
Rochdale	11–16/14–18
St Helens*	11–16/13–18
Suffolk East*	11–14/14–18
Wakefield	11–16/13–18 s.t.
Waltham Forest	11–14/14–18
†Wiltshire	11–16/13–18 s.t.
	11–14/14–18

* appears also in another category.

s.t. short term only.

† approved scheme covers only part of the area.

(D) *Authorities with VIth Form Colleges approved* (19)

Cardiff	Lincolnshire (Lindsey)
Cornwall	Luton
Darlington	Nottinghamshire
Dewsbury	Preston
Eastbourne	Redbridge
Essex	Rotherham
Hampshire	Southampton
Huddersfield	Stoke on Trent
Herefordshire	Tynemouth
Lancashire	

A Glossary of Educational Terms

ALL-AGE SCHOOL: A school containing children of all ages from five to fifteen; those of secondary age will have failed to qualify for a grammar or technical school.

BILATERAL SCHOOL: A secondary school with two distinct sides: grammar/technical; or grammar/'modern'; or technical/'modern'.

CERTIFICATE OF SECONDARY EDUCATION (CSE): An examination intended for the majority of children (i.e. all except the most and least able) to be taken normally at sixteen. Grade One is equivalent to GCE 'O' level. It is administered by fourteen regional boards and largely controlled by teachers. Each school decides whether its syllabuses and methods of assessment shall be mainly internal or mainly external.

COLLEGE OF EDUCATION (Training College): A college for the education and training of teachers, mainly or entirely non-graduate teachers aged eighteen or over, who study for three years for the Certificate in Education. Minimum admission qualification is five 'O' levels. A minority (from five to twenty-five per cent in different areas) take the B.Ed. degree after a fourth year.

COMPREHENSIVE SCHOOL: A school taking practically all the children from a given district (i.e. all apart from the educationally subnormal, the physically handicapped, and those attending independent schools) and not organized in distinct sides. The maintained primary schools of England and Wales (normal age range five to eleven) are thus comprehensive primary schools. The term 'comprehensive school' is, however, more usually applied to secondary schools which take practically all local school children aged eleven to nineteen. Recently it has been more loosely used, e.g. in the Crowther Report and by the Inner London Education Authority, to indicate schools which provide suitable courses for a wide range of ability but which do not necessarily take practically all local children.

COUNTY COLLEGE: An institution to be provided by a local education authority under the 1944 Education Act, for compulsory, part-time attendance by young people under eighteen who are not in full-time attendance at a school or other educational institution. No county colleges have yet been provided. A broader concept has been suggested by the present author in *Comprehensive Education: A New Approach*, and in the present work.

DAY RELEASE: The arrangement by which employers allow certain workers time off without loss of pay, usually for one day a week, to study at a college of further education.

DIRECT-GRANT GRAMMAR SCHOOL: A school which is not under the control of the local education authority but which receives a financial grant direct from the Ministry of Education. This grant is at present £32 a year per pupil below the sixth form and £116 in the sixth form. To qualify for grant, the school must provide free places, to the extent of at least twenty-five per cent of its intake, to pupils who have spent at least two years in a maintained primary school. The school charges fees to other pupils, who may be admitted to the school's own primary department from the age of seven-plus.

DIVISIONAL EXECUTIVE: An *ad hoc* body for a particular district set up in accordance with the 1944 Education Act to deal with the day-to-day administration of primary and secondary education, and some aspects of further education, within the framework of the overall policy laid down by a county council, from which its delegated powers are derived.

ELEMENTARY SCHOOL: Before 1944, elementary education – concentrating very largely on the 'three Rs' (reading, writing and arithmetic) – was provided by voluntary bodies or by designated local authorities for children aged from five to fourteen who did not attend the fee-charging secondary schools.

ELEVEN-PLUS: The examination and selection procedure used by a local education authority to find a basis on which to allocate children leaving primary schools about the age of eleven to different types of secondary education.

EXCEPTED DISTRICT: Where the town council of a borough or urban district is designated as a Divisional Executive, this area is described as an Excepted District. Excepted Districts usually have rather more powers delegated from the county council than has an ordinary Divisional Executive.

FURTHER EDUCATION: Education for people who have left school. The official term does not include universities.

GENERAL CERTIFICATE OF EDUCATION (GCE): A certificate awarded as the result of a national examination, set by any one of eight examining boards. A candidate – who need not be attending a school – may sit for any number of subjects. There are no age restrictions, but in schools the Ordinary level is customarily taken about the age of sixteen in from one to ten subjects, and the Advanced level about the age of eighteen, in from one to four subjects.

GRADUATE TEACHER: A teacher holding a university degree. A graduate is regarded as a qualified teacher even though he may not have taken the optional one-year training course for the Graduate Certificate in Education. If, however, a graduate takes this training course and fails, he may lose the teaching qualification which he had before he embarked on the course.

GRAMMAR SCHOOL: A secondary school providing a mainly academic course from eleven to sixteen or eighteen. It is the main route to the universities and the professions. Grammar schools maintained by local education authorities are of three kinds:

1. *County schools* entirely provided by the LEA.
2. *Voluntary-controlled* schools originally provided by a voluntary body such as a church, but now entirely financed and controlled by the LEA, which supplies two-thirds of the school's governing body.
3. *Voluntary-aided* schools originally provided by a voluntary body which still maintains the fabric of the building but which relies on the LEA for all running expenses. The LEA supplies one-third of the governing body.

HIGH SCHOOL: In America, a comprehensive secondary school. The term is sometimes used in this sense in England, but it is also often applied to a girls' grammar school.

INDEPENDENT SCHOOL: A school which receives no money from public funds, and which therefore charges fees and may also have private endowments. All independent schools must be registered with the Department of Education and Science and conform to prescribed minimum standards. In addition, schools may apply for inspection by Her Majesty's Inspectors in order to be 'recognized as efficient'.

INSTITUTE OF EDUCATION: A federal institution, or Area Training Organization, normally financed through a university but representing the bodies mainly concerned with teacher training in the area: university colleges of education, teachers, local education authorities, and the Department of Education and Science. It oversees the academic and professional work of the constituent colleges and university department of education for certificates and diplomas, co-ordinates and helps to provide in-service education for experienced teachers, and recommends the granting of the status of qualified teacher by the Secretary of State for Education and Science. There are twenty Institutes for England and Wales.

IQ: 'Intelligence Quotient', or a child's intelligence rating compared with the average for his age and expressed as a percentage (the average being 100). It is determined by specially devised 'intelligence tests'.

LOCAL EDUCATION AUTHORITY (*LEA*): The county council or county borough council responsible for providing and administering primary, secondary, and further education in its area.

MAINTAINED SCHOOL: A school provided, controlled or aided by the local education authority.

'MODERN' SCHOOL: A maintained secondary school for children not selected for grammar or technical schools.

MULTILATERAL SCHOOL: A secondary school with three or more distinct sides, e.g. grammar, technical, and 'modern'. There are now no multilateral schools in England and Wales.

PREPARATORY SCHOOL: An independent school, age range usually between seven and fourteen, which prepares boys or girls for entry to 'public' schools *via* the Common Entrance examination (for independent schools) taken at thirteen.

PRIMARY EDUCATION: Education up to the age of about eleven, covering nursery schools or classes (two to five), infant school or department (five to seven), and junior school or department (seven to eleven).

'PUBLIC' SCHOOL: The term is not capable of exact definition, but it is most commonly applied to the bigger or more famous independent boys' boarding schools, about eighty in number, whose heads are members of the 200-strong Head Masters' Conference. The less well-known schools whose heads are members of H.M.C. are usually referred to as 'minor public schools'. A 'public' school is not public in any normal sense: it is not maintained by public funds, nor is it open by right to the children of the public.

SECONDARY EDUCATION: Education from about eleven to fifteen (the end of compulsory schooling) and upwards to a normal limit of nineteen-plus. Before 1944, however, it was not as now the second main stage in education, but a superior type of education for some children (mainly fee-payers) aged seven to eighteen, organized separately from elementary education.

SETTING: Re-grouping of the classes of a given year into 'sets' of roughly equal ability for a particular subject.

SIXTH FORM: The upper section of a secondary school, normally entered at fifteen or sixteen after taking some subjects at the Ordinary level of GCE, and preparing for Advanced level in from one to four subjects. Some pupils also prepare for university scholarships. Comprehensive schools are increasingly in their sixth forms providing courses in non-academic subjects.

SPECIAL SCHOOL: A school for children who are physically or mentally handicapped.

STREAMING: Grouping of the children of each year's intake into classes according to their general ability. Thus ninety children would be divided into three classes of thirty each: A (above average); B (about average); C (below average).

TECHNICAL SCHOOL: A secondary school giving a general course with technical bias up to sixteen or eighteen. Commonly took the second layer of general ability, as indicated by the eleven-plus examination, after the top layer had been selected for grammar schools.

TRIPARTITE SYSTEM: An ugly phrase for an ugly arrangement: the division of secondary education into grammar, technical, and 'modern' schools.

Index